THE
RIVER
IS US

THE RIVER IS US

Bill Stokes

NorthWord
PRESS, INC

Minocqua, Wisconsin

To our children
and their children.

Edited by Greg Linder
Designed by Patricia Bickner Linder
Cover photograph by Barbara Gerlach

Published by: NorthWord Press, Inc.
P.O. Box 1360
Minocqua, Wisconsin 54548

For a free catalog describing NorthWord's line of nature books and gifts, call 1-800-336-5666.

Library of Congress Cataloging-in-Publication Data

Stokes, Bill, 1931–
    The river is us / by Bill Stokes.
        p.   cm.
    ISBN 1-55971-214-7 : $9.95
    1. Natural history. 2. Nature. 3. Seasons. I. Title
QH81.S864   1993
508–dc20   93-10917
                                                        CIP

Printed in U.S.A.

About the Author

Bill Stokes received his journalism degree from the University of Wisconsin at Madison in 1958. In subsequent years, he worked for several Wisconsin newspapers—the *Stevens Point Daily Journal,* the *Wisconsin State Journal,* and the *Milwaukee Journal.*

Since 1982, Stokes has written a monthly column for the *Chicago Tribune.* He has published a number of magazine articles and four previous books, *Ship the Kids on Ahead, Hi-Ho Silver Anyway, Slapshot,* and *You Can Catch Fish.* Stokes grew up on a farm, and prefers to spend his time close to nature. He and his wife Betty live in Madison, enjoy traveling, and often retreat to their cabin near a trout stream in central Wisconsin.

TABLE OF CONTENTS

Spring

Summer

Autumn

Winter

Spring

EARTH'S VEINS

Now the rivers run dark with the tired old blood of another winter. They drain the land of the used and the soiled in a spectacular kind of dialysis, and the grand opportunity for everything to be fresh and clean is presented again.

Rivers have been doing this essential task for eons. We take their work for granted, as we do the rising of the sun. And we are only now beginning to emerge from an era of unspeakable river abuse, when these waterways became sewers for the poisons of industry and the refuse of our lifestyle.

But if it is our inclination now to lift some of the offensive burden from the rivers, there is also the underlying tendency to ignore them, to channel out their bends and bridge them out of sight with superhighways and streets, and even to reverse their flow. Except for an occasional flood, they acquiesce to our heavy-handed demands.

Now is a good time to reassess that insulting attitude. The early spring is a good time to go to the rivers, to note in their swirling eddies and back currents a reflection of our own being, and to see in their eternal flow the one-way pattern of life that we are a part of.

The first framework of summer is built in the early spring along the rivers. In the black muck of the riverbanks the leaves of skunk cabbage unfold like a green salad, hastening to collect their share of the spring sun before it is cut off by the alder and the dogwood.

Overhead, the great business of tree budding goes on in the river valleys. The willow take on a yellow tinge, and the maple blush a deep red, as if embarrassed at being caught naked in this warming time. Taken as a whole, the subtle, gentle colors of spring along the rivers are equally as beautiful as the more spectacular fall display.

Until we prove otherwise, wood ducks must be credited with a greater sense of style and class than their duck brothers and sisters, because they are drawn to the rivers as butterflies to flowers. They do their twisting honeymoon dances over the crisp air of the winding rivers, landing ridiculously high overhead on tree branches to look at each other, ducks in love.

They will settle down somewhere in a hollow tree, sub-letting space from the squirrels, to raise a family with the expertise and dedication of scientists.

The river valleys are concert halls of birdsong now. Territorial claims are being filed with whistles, squeaks, squawks, and screeches. It is like tune-up time for the grand symphony to follow, and there is a compelling invitation to take a seat and stay for it all.

The rivers, of course, are joined in an intricate network that serves every last square inch of Earth, and to deny them their due is the ultimate folly. They are as essential to us as the blood in our veins, and though they function with a composite harmony beyond our comprehension, we can at least acknowledge their presence in the early spring.

Go to a river. It will be a tonic for your system.

THAT MARCH

That March followed the great snows, when the giant tractor with the clanking tracks had come roaring down the narrow country road, its pointed, shiny plow pushing huge chunks of rock-hard snow out against the whips of willow and dogwood. Only a machine of such traction and power could force its way through the mountainous drifts, and from the top of Peterson's hill we had seen it crawling toward us, a strange yellow monster born of a suffocating winter.

Each day we had climbed the waves of winter's frozen surf to transgress the cold, bloodless sanctity of that season and to get safely home before it sucked us into the vortex of its long, dark night. And then the snowplow had come to slice through the drifts and make a tunnel of the road; and the drivers had stopped to wave and grin at us and to make sure that we stood clear of the long, glistening, silver-colored blades.

That March had a lot to do, collapsing those towering snow banks where we walked as children, shrinking them slowly so that cold little rivers ran out from under them until the ridges of snow were hollow and treacherous to climb.

That March brought the jackrabbits back to earth, pulling the thick rug of snow out from under them and handing them a betrayal of sorts, as their white coats made them stand out like bright blots against the slowly emerging fields of black and brown.

That March Herman Schranz carried us across the flooded road one sunny afternoon. My sister and I in turn climbed onto his back, and he walked through the rushing, knee-deep torrent of meltwater, poking at it with a stout wading stick and depositing us on the home side of the flood. Then he smiled and waved, and we slogged off through the slush and mud of that warm, vaporous day.

That March a muskrat crossed the road in front of us down near the cattail slough, and I tormented it until it stood its ground and then could be interpreted as an attacker. So I killed it with a rock and carried it home by its flat, rat-like tail, where my father pulled its hide off as easily as you would peel a banana.

That March the dog waited by the mailbox on the end of the driveway, as he always did, and when he saw us coming down the hill he ran to meet us, wagging and whining and making us feel important and loved.

That March on the way home from town, a tie-rod dropped off the steering mechanism of the old Chevrolet, and it eased gently over onto its side in one of the melting snowbanks like a big old pig going to bed. Forever thereafter, the footprint of Louie Lancaster, the hired man, was part of the upholstery up near the dome light.

That March the neighborhood cats gathered beneath a bedroom window, and in the howling and snarling of sorting out their loves, they made a shambles of juvenile sleep. Their caterwauling put fire to the imagination, and in the dark of night it became unmanageable and painful, and dictated a whimpering recourse.

That March a mouse somehow caught its tail in a mouse trap and dragged the device around in the darkened bedroom until terror replaced sleep; and finally Dad got up and came into the room to do what had to be done to the mouse, and to try to resurrect the shattered tranquillity of youthful innocence.

That March was mean and unpredictable, and it kept you off balance, until sometimes there was an inclination to scream a little. Marches are like that.

The Flight of the Chipmunk

A grand impatience sweeps the land now: Spring, it seems, has never been so recalcitrant, so downright ornery, so fraught with unpleasantness.

Or has it? Aren't most springs that way? Don't they all torment us with brief early warmth and sunshine that starts our sap flowing? And then don't they always clamp on the lid of endless gray days, ladling out periods of bitter cold and burying us in sodden snow until we teeter on the edge of total despair? Don't all springs do that?

Of course. But this current one, despite its moments, seems particularly objectionable, like a honeymoon with in-laws.

A contrary spring like this one tends to generate what seems like foolhardy behavior. How else can you explain the robins arriving just ahead of a snowstorm that makes them sit around like grumpy stockholders at a bankruptcy? And what possible reason can there be for male blackbirds showing up in the frozen marshes amid last year's ragged cattails, where they try to act as if they knew what they were doing?

And wouldn't it be interesting to interview a sandhill crane when it spirals down out of an early spring sky and sends its magnificent trumpeting call out over the cold, frozen marsh swamp, like God's bugle?

"So, Mr. Crane, you have wintered in the south and now you have returned to spend the summer with us. But the summer is months away, so why in the name of avian timetables did you come back when the frogs are still down in the frozen mud and the local turkeys are incubating snowballs?"

The impatience permeates every house and

household, from bedroom to attic and even inside the walls, where chipmunks have taken up rent-free residence. Occasionally you hear them in the winter, apparently settling into more comfortable sleeping positions.

Unlike their hosts, the chipmunks are too smart to venture forth during the winter, so they snooze through all of the elemental misery, and wake up only when spring kicks off its shenanigans. Even then, the chipmunks are very cautious and conservative, like mice in a new house, and you rarely see them until all the snow is gone and the days are warm enough for crow romance.

But like the pubescent kid who strips to the waist on the way home from school, or the macho dude who puts his convertible car top down, there apparently comes a time when the chipmunk's patience with spring is exhausted, so it simply goes ahead and does something foolish.

There doesn't seem to be any other way to explain why one of "our" chipmunks ventured out onto the last melting snow to lunch on sunflower seeds beneath the bird feeder.

Oh, you could speculate that the chipmunk had been looking at the seeds from the shelter of the house, and it hadn't had a square meal since last fall, when potato chips were spilled under the picnic table. And you could imagine that the chipmunk figured that if the sparrows and juncoes could dine out there without incident, it would be safe for him. (Somehow spring foolishness seems to have a male bias.)

The more likely circumstance is, however, that the chipmunk got so impatient with the miserable spring that it just said, "Oh the devil with it, I'm going out to get some of those sunflower seeds."

That was a bad decision. No sooner had the chipmunk settled in for some serious seed eating than down out of the sky came the resident cooper's hawk, and with barely a pause, it clutched the chipmunk in its talons and flew off behind the neighbor's house.

This is not a pleasant story from the chipmunk family's point of view, and it encourages some anthropomorphic eavesdropping:

"Has anyone seen Uncle Chippy?"

"Yeah, he flew off with a hawk."

"Do tell! Where was he going?"

"He didn't say."

There's an obvious message here: Don't let your impatience with spring drive you to do something foolish.

On the other hand, how else could a chipmunk ever experience the thrill of flight?

Spring in the South

Spring, the real spring with days of blossoms and nights of frogs, is now down around the lower Mississippi River, where it is building up a head of steam for its run up the river and across the breadth of the country.

On the New Orleans waterfront, just up from where the tour boats dock, a calliope flings ragged clouds of sound and vapor at the warming wind, and over the levee, tourists pause to eat beignets and drink coffee au lait. The sun is warm on their backs, like a strange magnetic force that dissolves the dregs of winter from their bodies and makes tulip beds of their minds.

Metaphoric excess? Well, spring is a time for excess: more flowers than you can see, more birdsong than you can hear, more passion for renewal than you can endure.

Spring uses biology to make fools of us all. And we love it. The season is for the young, but who is not young when the earth does its spring tilt and the flow of sap is not unique to the maple trees of the North?

In the Deep South, the azalea bushes are like torches around the houses. The colors are just as bright beside the shacks as they are in the yards of the mansions, as spring demonstrates its spirit of sublime equality.

Wisteria vines do their lavender and white embraces with the abandon of partying uncles, and the building or tree that is so engulfed must know the ambivalence of smothering glory.

Blossoming redbud trees are everywhere, like blushing guests; and in the woods, lacy clouds of dogwood blossoms float on the breeze like the ghosts of departed rebels, gone but not forgotten, never forgotten.

Tender green leaves unfold by the millions each

moment, and there is something sensual and sexy about it: gently swaying wood nymphs in a dance of green veils; a tender, teasing come-on from an old pro who knows of our weaknesses.

Halfway up the Mississippi River, with that botanical tidal wave thundering along in magnificent silence, there is a freak snowstorm. It pulls the rug out from under anyone with the audacity to try to travel with spring. There is something about the season that discourages accompaniment, a subtle message: "Do not come to me, I will come to you, in due time and on my terms."

So now, further north, we all wait. And while the forsythia may blaze around us, and the crocus may appear, spring has not really arrived yet. It is still partying down in New Orleans. But it is on the way. If you listen carefully, you can hear the faint tones of the steam calliope, and you can smell the sweet aroma of a billion blossoms.

THE GREEN CURTAIN

There is something backward about this time of year from an audience standpoint: The green curtain comes down, and behind it the greatest natural dramas of life and death are played out.

Now, unseen behind new leaves and lacy blossoms, every creature renews its evolutionary claim to a piece of the earth.

There is a certain frenzy about it, a shrillness. You can hear it in the birdsong when the first light of day rolls from east to west with a tidal wave of sound. We know that the songs are not musical expressions of exhilaration, but rather "shouts and screams" to register territorial deeds.

It is appropriate accompaniment for the intense players behind the green curtain. In thickets and burrows and hollow trees, there is such incubating and hatching and birthing and growing that applause seems due, even from an audience denied.

Occasionally, there are little hints of what goes on behind the curtain. A flightless young robin, fat and dumb, appears inexplicably on the lawn. A fawn somehow misses a motherly cue and stands in wide-eyed wonder beside a country road. In the night there is a brief screech of terror as a young rabbit dies in the clutches of an owl.

There is a lot of dying in the unseen spring drama. The young of one species goes to feed the young of another. An adult blue jay hunts with a plaintive whine that elicits the response of the cardinal's hungry young, and the food transaction of abduction and "murder" is done as neatly as you would buy a hamburger.

There are tremendous heroics when timid mothers as fragile as butterflies fling themselves in the face of aggressors a hundred times their size. Sometimes you see this part of the drama if you inadvertently become the "aggressor." Birds swirl about your head if you get too close to their nest.

But these are just little peeks at what is really going on. We miss most of the show behind the green curtain.

Yet we can assume some things: As much dying as there is on the wild stage, there is more living. And ultimately there is a happy ending. It is in the numbers which guarantee that the cycle will repeat itself, and if we are lucky, we will be in the audience next time the green curtain comes down.

THE SURVIVAL GAME

A black cat, on little fog feet, cuts across a corner of the back yard. It goes at a dichotomous pace—with the graceful hesitation step of a bride and exhibiting the assured demeanor of a deputy sheriff.

At the bird feeder, a cardinal pauses in its gluttonous consumption of sunflower seeds and looks at the cat. Then it flies off to perch in the bare branches of the honeysuckle, there to contemplate its uninvited dinner companion.

The cardinal has survived the long, cold winter and the chilly days of early spring, and now its red presence is a blue chip in the big survival game of competing species.

The cat does not look at the cardinal—another day, perhaps, as the bird continues to convert sunflower seeds into something more palatable to a fussy cat, and when the cat's appetite has not been satisfied by canned food provided by the great American industrial complex. Out of that can, of course, has come a subliminal life insurance policy for the cardinal that the bird can appreciate no more than it appreciates the sunflower seeds, but which illustrates the pervasive and subtle influence of man in the grand scheme.

High over the scenario of the cat and the cardinal, skeins of geese cleave the late afternoon sunshine. They come in wavering lines and V's—like a surrealistic script delivering the subconscious message of the ages. Their cries bounce on the eardrums like tiny, jigging parasites, causing itches for which there is no satisfying scratch, and making a mockery of intellectual smugness.

The afternoon wears on, the sky a cold blue that has used a northwest wind all day long to fend off the warmth of the sun.

Blue jays come to the feeder, feathered bullies spoiling for confrontation. They eat and run, like a raucous gang on a beer break. Their patrol has chased the cardinal, and the cat has disappeared behind a neighbor's storage shed.

Off to the west, the setting sun is like spilled paint. A spectacular flood of pink and lavender and yellow flows up from a center of fiery red. It turns darker and then it fades, and it is like a great signal of transition, of the day and the season.

As if in response, the moon rises off the eastern horizon, balloon-like and pale. Slowly it is transfused by the darkness, until it assumes the authority needed to prevail like a security guard over the night and the suspended activity of spring.

The earth rotates and the planets retain their eternal positions, and in the morning, at first light, the cardinal assumes its perch in the topmost branch of the tallest tree, and its call is a celebration of survival and of the cycle.

Somewhere, the cat sleeps.

A Fine Crop of Gulls

Now in this season of grand planting, the genetic residue of "farmer" ancestors must stir in the bones of everyone. Even the city sophisticate, who uses a peculiar arrogance to deny ties to the earth, must experience inexplicable surges of energy with the warming of the land.

This energy is born of the universal urge to participate in the glory of spring with all of the other life forms; to stifle it frustrates your system as surely as the postponement of a sneeze.

For millions of people, resisting the agrarian spring urges is unthinkable: The sun mounts higher, the earth warms, and so they must plant.

Farmers guide massive tractors across the prairie, leaving freshly turned soil in their wake and dominating the landscape as it has never been dominated down through the ages. Back and forth the machines go, like new-age dinosaurs, domesticated and trained to straight lines and a steady gait.

Gardeners nurse tender young plants with parent-like concern. On their hands and knees, they inhale the timeless aromas of the soil, and something deep within them knows a mysterious satisfaction.

Those who don't get directly involved can exercise their attachment to the natural harmony of spring and its botanical beginnings by pausing to admire the delicate shading of budding trees, or by becoming suddenly aware that the view out the window is different—green and soft, like the gateway to an enchanted land.

For all of us there are the memories of other springs, sprouted from the seeds of our unique experiences and grown to become the blossoms of our little bouquets of time. There was a field, isolated by trees and next to a marsh where mallards paired off with the intensity of duelists. On a spring day, while the tractor droned back and forth in rural solitude, a flock of seagulls appeared suddenly. Gulls never came to these fields, but there they were—regal, white and carrying wondrous messages of other worlds to a boy who rode the tractor and was so conditioned to the importance of spring planting that if it had not been for the gulls, his childish dreaming might have been impaired.

The gulls stayed for a time and then flew off toward Lake Superior, 100 miles to the north. Of all the things that were planted that spring, the seeds for the memory of the gulls produced the most enduring crop. It continues to produce, and now in this spring it will be supplemented with something new.

Spring planting is that way: You never know just how you will participate. But nobody gets left out, and that is the wonder of it.

THE CHICK AND WORM SHOW

Now in these days of lengthening sunlight, when the land lies still and cold—the brown botanic corpse of other seasons—I join the chickens in lamenting the fact that the brooder house has gone the way of the outhouse.

Contrary to what you might think, a brooder house is not, or was not, a home for disgruntled and pouting philosophers. It was a building, usually small, tightly constructed and with generous south-facing windows, in which freshly hatched chicks were nurtured and nourished in a manner designed to duplicate the efforts of the mother hens that it replaced.

Critical to its successful operation, of course, was heat: Chicks fresh out of the eggs are as vulnerable to cold as wet babies. Most brooder house heaters had a metal canopy under which the chicks clustered, perhaps genetically curious about the replacement of a mother's warm fluffy feathers by galvanized tin and a light bulb, but displaying no obvious dismay over the exchange.

The chicks' lives seemed adequate, if not happy, and I make this assessment with some authority: As a farm boy striving mightily to pluck an occasional frayed thread from the mysterious tapestry of life, I spent a considerable amount of time in the brooder house with the chicks. On the heels of a long, cold winter, it was a warm and cozy place to pass idle hours; and the mass of tiny, yellow chicks was a constant source of entertainment—like a microcosm of society, with feeding habits and little feuds and a pecking order that seemed fragile and ridiculous.

And into this chicken culture, a peculiar kind of very entertaining chaos could be generated by the introduction of a few earthworms. With frost still squeezing the earth in a steel-hard grip, worms were difficult to come by, but a resourceful kid could always find a few next to the barn foundation or under the garden mulch.

With apologies to the worms, it was a wonderful show when one of them was tossed onto the brooder house floor. After a second or two of hesitation, one of the bright-eyed chicks would snatch the worm up in its beak and the battle would be joined. Other chicks, spotting the dangling worm, would give chase and a kind of hilarious puffball Keystone Cops scene would ensue.

Attracted by the commotion, other chicks would join in, and there would be a tumbling, zig-zag gang pursuit of the chick with the worm. Invariably, a dangling worm end would be grabbed by a second chick and perhaps even a third, and teetering tugs-of-war would break out, to be replaced by more chasing and more struggling.

Eventually, the worms would be divided up and devoured, and peace would return to the flock. The chicks would reassemble in the warmth under the canopy and, peeping contentedly, doze and rest in the uninhibited nature of the very young.

Then in the lull you could contemplate the larger questions, such as: How did the chicks, without benefit of teaching from a mother hen, know that worms were good to eat? And, if such valuable information can be passed on through genes, why didn't I know at birth about such things as ice cream and chocolate candy?

Such "brooding" questions were never meant to be answered. It was enough to contemplate them in warm privacy, perhaps as a late blizzard whispered outside and smacked the windows with wet, snowy kisses.

Permit this retrospective observation: While visual entertainment may have been hard to come by in the dark ages before TV, particularly in rural areas as winter expired with stormy gasps, I'll wager that the brooder house shows could still draw today—perhaps only audiences of one, but that seems to be about the right size.

THE DOGS OF SPRING

The spectacular pasque flower is gone from the sandy roadside, its delicate structure lost to the season, and now the lupine emerges in lush blue patches. Back in the woods, beautiful moccasin orchids bow to the warming breezes, and ferns send their graceful fronds out to gather sunshine in the developing shade.

And in the fresh spring green beside the road, the big dog looked up from where it crouched, its bloody muzzle suspended over the mangled fawn like the precision apparatus of a butcher. The dog lay curled in the softness of new grass and sedge as if it were nesting, one of its front paws outstretched over the ripped flesh, and its farm-dog eyes as matter of fact as a shopper's. This is my fawn, the eyes said. I caught it and killed it, and now it is my lunch.

Well, bon appetit, country dog, but you shouldn't have done that. There are laws, you know, about dogs running loose and killing things. If you want the warmth of our campfire, you bastard wolf of domesticity, you must learn that killing other creatures is ordained only for purposes of human commerce and entertainment. As far as you are concerned, it is the ultimate obedience school: Sit! Stay! Thou shalt not kill! Eat your Alpo! Nice doggy!

One spring, in another place, it was sheep and lambs, and then there was a furious uproar in the neighborhood. The talk moved through—from farm to farm, like the cold tail of a late spring storm whipping up trouble. Stray dogs, people said. Maybe a pack of them. Wild, like wolves. Vicious killers.

Then the farm women watched their bug-eyed children and made them play close to the house, and the men gathered in yards with rifles under their arms and their farmer caps pulled down like the Stetsons of aggrieved deputies.

The men waited one night in the cold starlight, their voices whispering from behind the skeletons of fence-line cherry and willow, and their calloused hands holding the rifles like wands. They heard nothing, but when the morning mists lifted off a far corner of the pasture, pieces of a lamb were scattered as if in a game.

Another night the attack came in an adjoining pasture, and the sheep fled in a heedless stampede until they ran into the wire fences and injured themselves.

Then the spring talk took its own leaps and bounds, of mysterious creatures and cat-like beasts, and the children were drawn in even closer to the houses.

Finally one night the waiting paid off, and the attack came in a pasture where the men could see the dark shapes slink along close to the ground until the sheep began to run, nervously at first, then in a plunging mass. And then the rifles stabbed little slashes of fire into the night and shotguns boomed and later, in the cold light of the morning, the truth was known: The men had shot some of their own dogs and the dogs of their neighbors.

It had been spring sport for those gentle, obedient pets that curled in the front-porch sunshine by day, greeting the family with great wagging and licking the faces of the babies. Then at night they had gathered like their ancient ancestors, trotting out from dens on neighboring hillsides; they had forgotten that stifling compact with Man and become once again their own creatures, predatory pack animals obeying genetic commands to pursue and kill.

The spring's invitation to regression is not peculiar to dogs. Somehow it seems to lie on the green bosom of this season like the ultimate temptation. Now is the time when the earth explodes with growth; and in the descent of the great green curtain, old roles come slithering out of nowhere. It is the gentle craziness, and there can be no harm in obeying the urge to sit cross-legged among the wild flowers like a simple, satiated simian.

The Wind Speaks

Now the wind sweeps the land with a seasonal broom of bluff and bluster. It slips across the prairie, rearranging bits of dried vegetation in the stubble fields, and it moves in hissing frustration where plows have buried the debris of last year and turned the earth into shiny black corduroy.

The wind dances along the fence line like a gang of boys playing hooky, tugging at last year's bird nests, bending branches and twigs, kicking at the clumps of grass where rodents hide, and moving on, always moving on, as restless as youth.

In the woods, the wind choreographs a flow of motion that makes the dance of the trees a spectacular thing. No stage has ever known such a show.

And now the wind can reach down through the bare branches and sift through the clutter of leaves and needles on the forest floor, rustling, sighing, whispering. The wind speaks with its most refined tone when it brushes through the pine. Then you can hear in it the voice of the ages, gossip from grandfathers, lullabies of mothers, the gentle hissing tease of time.

In the marshes, the wind is welcomed with a million ragged banners. And then slowly the cattails dissolve, like seasonal popsicles licked away by tongues of wind, and the seeds of future crops are spread to every possible niche of dampness.

Within days the first blackbirds will arrive—eager males that must question their biological clocks when the wind blows in the inevitable spring blizzards.

And the blizzards will come, soggy and swirling, blocking roads and sidewalks, delighting children and even some adults. Then the wind is at its best, seeming to move the very surface of the earth in undulating waves, bending the trees, obscuring images, and poking and splattering with the wet snow until all things are either buried or wrapped in white.

Without things to move, the wind passes as a silent, invisible force that has no character. But give it the snow or the ragged land or open water, and it can become a romantic whisper, a riotous party, a thunderous assault.

It is never the lakes that threaten us with watery fangs. It is the wind. It seems to delight in splashing great heaps of cold water in the face of social sophistication and its symbols of power.

The wind is perhaps the last voice of nature to speak the message that no matter the height of the dwellings or the degree of species arrogance, no atom of anything can drop out of the natural drama.

Now in this season, we listen to the wind, under the pine or on the lakeshore. It is everywhere, and though its message can rattle our bones and addle our brain, we hear it with a welcome reverence that comes mysteriously to our consciousness.

Between a Tree and a Beaver

Snowbanks still clung to the north slopes on that Arbor Day. They were the crystallized remains of an ugly winter that had crushed the north country with more than the usual burden of cold and snow.

But the late April day had dawned as fresh as meltwater, and now in the afternoon a ragtag bunch of country kids sloshed through the mud and melting snow along the Yellow River. Earlier, a teacher had dismissed them to go to the woods as part of an Arbor Day exercise, obviously giving silent thanks for an excuse to get them out of her hair, however briefly.

There was a special quality to the air, as if it had been washed in strong soap and rinsed repeatedly in the spring water that bubbled up here and there along the river banks. The day was like a flawless canvas, stretched to receive the work of a great artist. And here came the kids, as innocent as birds, as awkward as turtles: They were the artist.

They slipped and slid down the steep hill, where white pine stood like giant, green-robed monks; and they splashed their way along the swamp where last year's cattails hung like rags. They crossed the river on the bridge of popple poles, stopping to stare down into the black, swirling water and thinking their own thoughts about what it would be like to fall in.

They jumped on top of a brush pile until a cottontail rabbit came bounding out and bounced away like a yo-yo. And they peered up into the shadowy branches of a tall pine where giant killer cats would hide if they had not been extinct. But who could be sure of a thing like extinction?

Then they climbed through some of the crystal snow, and suddenly the spectacle was there before them: In a cruel twist of wind and wood, a giant cottonwood had slipped from its stump and landed squarely in the middle of a beaver's tail, pinning the animal to the ground as effectively as the most devious trap. The beaver had apparently been felling the tree and had gnawed through its thick trunk when the tree made its move, not falling with an echoing crash as the beaver had expected, but hopping off the stump and remaining upright to pin the beaver in a death trap.

The kids stood silently in the sodden debris of winter and stared at the dead beaver, at its bloated body and dull, sightless eyes. They thought about the agony the beaver must have known, and the helplessness of its situation. The instinctive engineering expertise of the animal and its colony had not been able to deal with such a complication, and the kids stood for a long time as that fact soaked into their sponge-like beings.

So now on Arbor Day, some of those "kids" remember the tree and the beaver that killed each other. And as was the case on that day so long ago, they do not affix any blame. It was just something that happened between a tree and a beaver.

Everywhere, the Young

Now the land is a great nursery and the young of a thousand species claim it for their own.

In the early morning, colts lie as flat and still as rugs on the green hillside, and the mares are over them in the mist like statues from an equine age.

In another pasture, where a tiny stream has placed a diamond necklace on the swelling bosom of spring, white-faced calves cavort, tossing their heads, running stiff-legged and switching their tails. Obviously, they have never been taught by their plodding mothers that play is foreign to the bovine character.

In the woods, fawns lie hidden in the ferns like stashed pastry—delicate, exquisite works, genetically frosted for camouflage and the discerning palate of survival.

In a low, grassy field near a remote marsh, two sandhill cranes stalk like skinny spies tiptoeing through landmines. Between them, a chicken-sized young one struggles and stumbles to keep up, accepting frequently proffered insect lunches, and growing at an astonishing rate.

Back in the pine grove, the first squawks from young crows ride the clean spring air like Bronx cheers in church. As shiny black adults, the crows will never be noted for the quality of their voices, but as hungry youngsters, their harsh croaks are particularly discordant.

The robin family in the back yard functions with the efficiency of a surgical team, the parents bringing food and the youngsters consuming it as if each minute threatens starvation.

Wrens scold, sparrows gossip, blue jays screech, and

catbirds whine from the honeysuckle. And everywhere there is an aura of incredible parenting, of acquiescence to a common command, a directive that transcends everything else. It is issued through the gullets of the helpless young and, reduced to its bare essential, it is this: "Feed me! Feed me! Feed me!"

Now the little girl fit into it all like one of those youngsters in a nearby nest. Her cheeks were flushed with sunshine and play, and her eyes flashed with the sheer joy of life. She came bursting into the cabin kitchen, a bundle of elbows and legs and flying hair, and she said, "Mom, I'm hungry!"

A peanut butter and jelly sandwich later, she was outside again, out with the colts and calves and fawns and birds. She was one of them, joined irrevocably to all of the other young by the invisible packaging of the future. Within her and within them, the ambitions and hopes of the body and the spirit repose like jewels.

FITTING IN

The premature heat of the season came down over the wild land like a blanket, as if it would smother and suffocate life in the great nursery of spring. But beneath it, the birth and hatching and emerging of millions of entities proceeded with such vigorous precision as to verge on chaos.

In the shadowy moistness, the regeneration and the renewal was a slow, undulating thing that transfused the senses with undecipherable fragments, with peripheral impressions and sensations, with the most subtle of phantom tugs from umbilical cords long severed.

There was, beneath the umbrella-like canopy of trees and in the impenetrable lushness of the thickets, an aura of beginnings, of your own and those of everything else, and of the steaminess and mystery in which they were wrought. You could, it seemed, reach out to touch the mercuric core of creation, and sense its tenuous position on the slippery slope up from the swamps.

It was all bound together, infinite strands woven into a swaddling cloth by a hot-fingered sun for the collective baby of what? Some of its pieces and parts of its progress—as with this spring—are not beyond us, but its beginning and its destiny elude us, and we are left to accept and to eternally wonder about the whole of it.

Within the seasonal whirl, the moves are as predictable as a square dance, and the confrontations as programmed as do-si-dos. There is the contest for sunlight, with some plants growing six inches or more in a single day and others spreading leaves as big as napkins. There are the trees reaching out to claim space for their leaves before their neighbors can make their moves. There are the insect hordes, feeding on each other and on everything else; countless birds singing claims to their private little domains; reptiles and amphibians, heated by the sun so that their personal engines are red-lined; and there are the warm-blooded mammals hidden away with their vulnerable young.

Now it is impossible to step out of the door without relating to some of it. Beneath the white pine and dogwood, exquisite moccasin orchids protrude up from the dead brown leaves like delicate lavender balloons; and along the country road, the lupine, spiderwort, wild geranium, phlox, columbine, and many other blossoming plants draw your attention as if you were a nectar-collecting bee. A half-dozen species of ferns provide just the right blend of greenery for the bouquet that goes on and on, and finally in the midst of the boundless wild beauty the point is made that since you are not a bee, your appreciation of it is not a factor, not in any meaningful sense anyway.

On one of those simmering afternoons, there was a sudden cracking in the treetops and a huge maple limb came crashing to earth. The weight of hundreds of new leaves and a quick little gust of wind had pruned it as neatly as a saw, and it lay there in the shade of its neighbors as a strange new/old corpse, its fresh lush leaves simultaneously alive and dead. That it was done in by its own overreaching seemed obvious, but conclusions about such things are anathema to the calculator who can never have a complete set of facts.

A deerfly manages to gouge a meal from the back of a hand, and though it pays with its life, its work lives on in the swelling and stiffness that its bite produces. Mosquitoes also come to leave their marks, and some of them, too, are crushed with sharp slaps. The insects are memorialized in the itching, and the confrontation with them was as programmed as all of the other actions and reactions.

A crow intercepts a mother squirrel as she moves one of her kits across a grassy area. The squirrel drops her youngster to fend off the crow, and the bird feints her away and quickly makes off with the baby squirrel, flying laboriously toward the tall pine where its nest is crowded with squawking young. It happens quickly, before a decision can be made to interfere.

The confrontations go on and on, most of them without benefit of human observation or participation. But then there are others: A tiny tree toad finds itself stuffed into a small boy's pocket, and struggles there briefly before it ends up in a fruit jar for the long ride to town. And even as this is written, a wood tick is plucked from the back of a knee, where it had set up camp.

There can be no doubt: We are as much a part of the grand scheme of spring as any other collection of cells.

THE RIVER PREVAILS

Sometimes in the spring, a pickerel comes up out of the river to haunt the trout holes in the creek. Its jutting, shovel-like snout points into the current, while its fins move slowly to hold its position; and its stiff, reptilian configuration disguises it as a dark log against the sand. Its large eyes are as hard as glass, and there is no way to see through their shiny darkness into the tiny brain that must accommodate so little: only the occasional torpedo-like lunge to impale a trout or a chub on the rows of needle teeth between the suddenly gaping jaws, or the hormonal directive in the early spring to seek the swampy shallows for procreation.

The river is busy in the spring, and it sends the pike on its mission as incidentally as it welcomes the blackbirds in the cattails and drains the meltwater down to a level that encourages the marsh marigolds and the frog songs of the spring peepers.

The river is something to everything. It is one of the crucial arteries to the beating of the earth's heart, and all life depends on it and relates to it. Some of the signs are plain: the sharp hoofprints in the black muck where the deer come to drink; the early-season dragonfly that hovers over the water to capture the first tiny insects; the wood duck that rides the current so secretively now in the proximity of the hollow oak where it nests.

Relationships to the river can sometimes be convoluted. Once in the late winter, the metabolic timing of a frog malfunctioned, and in a side eddy of the river beneath a layer of transparent ice, the frog swam stupidly and endlessly against the current, staying in the same place by dint of its efforts, but with no hope of improving its position.

A long time ago, on an isolated, paint-faded farm at the end of a sand road, an old man claimed a stretch of the river as his own. The river was his, he reasoned, because it was on his property, just like the trees and the rocks. And the fish were his, too—the trout that hide beneath the pasture banks and emerged to take hatching caddis flies with delicate little surface kisses.

And there was the rub, of course, because the uncaught fish cannot belong to anyone; and the river, by the law of navigation, was open to those who would canoe its route or wade its slithering flow.

But the old man lived by his own rules, shaking a thin, gnarled finger to make his point and stringing his words together with a nasal whine. And sometimes he would stand on the high bank like an animated scarecrow and throw rocks down at the rising fish until a fisherman could only give up and head on downstream. Once, along his hayfield on a hot summer day, his wife and grown son carried hay down to the stream and threw it into the pools, where a fisherman tried to match an afternoon insect hatch.

And on one memorable evening, a fisherman's car suddenly had two flat tires when it ran over a sharpened metal stake that had been driven into the wheel track of a public access road near the old man's farm. There could be little doubt about the origin of the stake, and all that was needed that warm evening was the quiet chuckle of the old man off in the shadows as the fisherman gave up his evening of fishing and began the long walk to get tire help.

The old man is gone now, dead probably, as mortal as any other life form along the river. And the stream is no different for his years of proprietary oversight. It runs through the alder and birch and in back of the dilapidated old farm buildings as it always did, and if there are any more trout in it by virtue of the old man's efforts, you could not prove that by the few anglers who come to it.

The river hosts the cycles of the simple and the complex: the caddis flies that live most of their lives beneath the surface, and as adults have undeveloped mouth parts and cannot feed, and so they mate and die; and the humans who sometimes come to play along the river, but who mostly ignore the stream as they cross over it on high-speed bridges.

The river prevails. All rivers prevail in one way or another, no matter the manipulation and the abuse. And to claim ownership or complete control of a river, or even to take one for granted, particularly now in the spring, when they all course with such authority and beauty, is an absurdity and an insult.

THE GRAND SUSPENSION

From the edge of the field, you could see spring unfolding like an old map. A surprise snow had melted to become glistening gems scattered across the brown stubble, and an ambitious sun pored over it all with the resolution of an omnipotent jeweler.

In the expectant hush of the bright afternoon, there was a grand hesitation, an acknowledgment of this precise time and place that stretched beyond the measure of clocks and calenders. It was a universal time-out, a brief denial of forces and cycles, an occasion of displaced cultural disciplines with life suddenly as sensory as young love.

To step from the cover of the oak and pine, and to stand still at the field's edge, was to be awed by the panorama and the circumstance of suspended mandates.

High overhead—so high that it took several seconds to see its form against the blue of the sky, a sandhill crane circled down out of a thermal and announced its presence with a series of wild yodels. The call, as always, came to earth as the reverberating voice of craziness, an aberrant cheer for something beyond comprehension; then it was answered from the field, where other cranes strode as regally as the emperor's guards.

Off to the left, a pair of tom turkeys sneaked back toward the jack pine, their heads low and their strange little beards dangling from their breasts. They now fill the mornings with sound just as outrageous as the cranes', and if now, in this sensory time, all those male sounds were gathered and interpreted, the cacophony would surely daunt the sexists among us.

Then from a corner of the woods, where old neighbor

Paul built the pasture fence for his sheep and then died before the next lambing, four deer stepped silently out of the shadows. They stood as still as ornaments as they tested the field with their big ears and eyes and their black noses. Satisfied finally that the form over near the jack pine was nothing more than an odd-shaped fence post, the deer eased their way into the stubble and began to feed. Frequently they would stop—sometimes only one or two of them but other times all four—to raise their heads high and test the wind for sounds or smells.

Slowly, very slowly, they worked their way closer, and so the stage was set for the little drama in the afternoon of suspended things, when the deer and I would stare at each other as the distance between us narrowed.

Countless other times it had happened this way, but almost always there had been the encumbrance of hunting, when the animals' approach had been measured against a clear path for a bullet, and the emotion was generated by the coursing of predatory blood.

A flock of geese flew overhead, their cries dropping down to the field like mourning; then the deer raised their heads and stared off in the direction of a barking farm dog.

Closer they came, until I could see their eyes and the blackness of their noses. And with their nearness, their perception sharpened, until it was increasingly difficult for them to mistake me for a fence post. For long moments the deer would stare, then with flicks of their tails go back to feeding in the sparse stubble, only to jerk their heads up again.

The suspension of the afternoon was raised to a new dimension in the odd stand-off, and into the breach tumbled thoughts of having killed and eaten the sires of these graceful creatures that now strolled so delicately before me.

Beyond them was the pasture fence where Paul's

sheep would be if he hadn't died, and there in the sunshine of spring—the time when lambs are born, there was time to consider the distinctive tastes of venison and mutton and their respective places on the cultural menu.

Then some wafting of a sliver of scent or an inadvertent movement alerted the deer. They stared, and one of them stomped a front leg nervously. And then in glorious, soaring leaps they were off, great white tails upraised and swaying as they bounded over the field and back into the woods.

The cranes set up an uproarious yodeling session, like the cheering section of a madhouse, as the deer disappeared.

And then the grand suspension collapsed in on itself.

The Strange Dog

It was the spring of the strange dog, and winter was dying with great soggy reluctance along the country road. Pussywillows were using their tiny gray tongues to ridicule the shrinking snowbanks, and the sharply pointed shoots of skunk cabbage had speared up here and there along the marsh.

The dog appeared first as a silhouette on a distant snow-covered hill. Its form was somehow alien to the landscape of between-season sterility, like a louse stranded on a cold corpse. It was there for only a minute, then it turned and dropped out of sight behind the hill.

Several days later, as we walked the muddy road home from school, the dog showed up again. This time it was closer, standing at the top of a snow cliff that had built over the crest of a knoll.

We called to it, our child voices sliding across the brushy pasture like the cries of wounded things, but the dog stood unmoving and stared at us. It was dark-colored and very skinny, and its shaggy coat was matted and dirty.

I left some bread crusts from my lunchbox on a snowbank. The next day they were gone, and the dog stared at us from a different location, this one close enough so that we could see in its eyes a hard wariness that seemed to transcend its mistrust of us as individuals and speak more to the species we represented.

A long time ago, the dogs came slinking up to our ancient campfires, probably to snitch bones and food scraps. A deal was struck: food for companionship, shelter for subservience, kindness for trust. It was called domestication, and in the case of dogs it took on the dimensions of an impassioned marriage. Dogs became "man's best friend" before there were words to describe the relationship.

But sometimes it doesn't work out, usually through no fault of the dog. On another spring, there was another dog. This one, too, was black and skinny, and it appeared suddenly on a dimly lighted industrial street hard by the railroad tracks. It slipped out from behind a battered dumpster, and it loped across the cracked asphalt as if its license to live had expired.

It glanced up briefly, then its head went down low again and it disappeared behind the corner of a warehouse, leaving a series of haunting sensory tracks.

The street dog provoked memories of the other dog, the one so long ago along the country road.

We saw that earlier dog several times after the first bread-crust incident, and each time it seemed to edge closer. But then one afternoon we heard the sharp crack of a rifle, and as we came over the hill, a car drove away. We heard the faint, shouting laughter of a young man, and the dog was nowhere to be seen.

Much later, after all of the snow had melted, we saw the crows circle down behind a thicket of hazel brush. And as country kids, we knew what that meant.

But we never went to look, to see if the crows were dining on the carcass of the dog. We didn't want to know for sure. Somehow we were too young to plug in to the great potential for cruelty that flutters like a bat in the soul of man.

I wish I were still too young, but there have been too many springs, and too many dogs.

A WALK WITH INNOCENCE

The early-spring night fit loosely on the wild land, like an unbuttoned jacket. The last of the darkness was gathering in the pine thickets, planning a retreat and a return, and the last stars winked conspiratorially.

An expectant hush prevailed, a punctuation in the passage of time. The nocturnal creatures had sought shelter and hiding for the daylight hours; the day creatures waited like a sophisticated audience for the downbeat of a familiar number.

And then it came, suddenly, almost rudely: the wild, uninhibited yodel of a sandhill crane. It rolled over the dawn like the perverse cackling of the devil, a ridiculous sound escaping like audio steam from deep down in the earth.

In its abruptness and volume, it functioned as an alarm clock that no hearing creature could deny. It is a sound that, once heard, is never forgotten; it reverberates in your bones like a strange voice left over from an age of grinding glaciers and thundering rivers.

The calling became louder as another crane joined the first to produce the magnificent unison call that is peculiar to the species.

And then the new day was officially born, welcomed like royalty and accepted as a returning loved one.

The day was encumbered with the usual baggage: demands for time, things to do. The cabin porch needs a new roof. The gate at the driveway has to be replaced. Down and broken trees need attention.

But later, in the midst of the demands and with the sun working its warm, motherly magic, nothing was more important than a walk with a granddaughter.

Jessy is at that wonderful age of innocence when each day is a package of delights, when skipping is a perfectly natural means of locomotion. Her six-year-old mind is like a ball that bounces everywhere, and you must be awed by your good fortune when it bounces your way.

Near the back-line fence, we saw the tracks of squirrels and raccoons and deer in the soft, damp ground.

Decaying ice and water covered the shallow slough, and Jessy rode piggyback across it. Near the far edge, the ice gave way and she giggled as the frigid water seeped into my boots and produced howling complaints.

We crossed the creek on a log and stopped by the spring for a drink. Jessy proclaimed it the best water she had ever had and, after a one-leaf sample, she expressed serious doubt about the palatability of watercress. Skunk cabbage, spearing up out of the black muck, impressed her, but mostly because of its name.

We returned through the meadow, then sat for a few minutes on the footbridge and talked about trout.

It was a day to make memories, maybe for Jessy and certainly for me. How could you ever forget a spring day that was born with such spectacular wild sound and peaked out so wonderfully in that walk with someone so special?

SOMETHING WRITHING

Something was writhing in the water-filled ditch, something slippery and glistening with wetness in the black meltwater of spring.

It was only a glimpse from the car, just a split second of seeing muscular, tentacle-like coils twisting and knotting together.

Was it a snake contorted in the capturing of a frog, or the snake itself caught in the jaws of a snapping turtle and struggling desperately for its freedom?

I'll never know, of course, because it was there and then it was gone. But it left this image, like a rubber stamp that is slammed down hard.

Over time, the image has transcended all natural and rational explanation to become something mysterious and illogical. It was, I imagine, a rare and flickering peek into the secret womb of the earth as it prepared for the great birth of spring. It was something I was not supposed to see, something in a backstage area that is forever closed to an audience of gawkers.

Spring is such a complex and explosive process, so exquisitely orchestrated, that we are taken with its spectacular props and its gaudy sets, and the soul of the show somehow escapes us.

It is like having gypsy flower girls and dancing clowns in the delivery room: The diversion is so awesome that the harmonious essence and the miracle of the wholesale rebirth go unrecognized.

Now that wondrous diversion is everywhere. Trees that stand through the year either bone-naked or draped in routine green have been for a brief period botanic sky-rockets, displaying such outrageous color as to encourage the conclusion that a production of this magnitude can be only a finale, and the big plants must now expire and disappear.

Flowers are everywhere, like an invasion of strange little soldiers in ridiculous but gorgeous dress uniforms. They pop up from the black muck of swamps, lean out over the trickling water of clear streams, and poke through the thick humus of the forest floor.

Once in a very remote woods, where the processes and cycles of life proceeded with marked success in the absence of humans, I stood beneath the leafing trees in a virtual sea of magnificent trilliums. Their white flowers, tinged with pink and lavender, stretched in all directions, and it was a humbling experience to know that I would be the only one to see them. It was further humbling to recognize that the trilliums would be no less beautiful if I had not happened along. There is something totally absurd in the arrogance of a species that considers the blossoming of a plant only in terms of the visual pleasure it presents.

That arrogance may blind us to the true mystery of spring, the mystery that goes beyond an understanding of the cellular processes and the very predictable botanic structures. Somewhere deep within us or deep within the earth there must be more to it, something beyond our reason or imagination that ties it all together in a way that we cannot comprehend.

Sometimes in the spring, when the earth is turned by a plow or excavated for a road or a basement, strange, pungent smells come to the senses, and the question is on the laden air like the ghostly wings of pterodactyls released suddenly from the grave of the ages: What great secret are we missing as the planet tilts and the cycles are all renewed?

We may never know the answer, and maybe there isn't one. But our role in the spring process must be enhanced simply because we pose the question.

The writhing in the watery ditch, my imagination says, might have been part of the answer. Then again, it might have been only a snake with a frog.

THE SEARCH

The grand search for summer places began earlier, during the first cold days of spring, when the land still lay in its winter pout. There was a subtleness to it, a soft fluttering by night, a quiet shuffling by day.

And now in May, as the earth warms beneath delicate bouquets, the search intensifies and spreads like a flood.

Geese that waited in the fields like a massed invasion force have scattered to the thawed marshes of the north, there to raise families in stirring isolation.

The blackbird mobs that seemed to have such a vivacious migratory party in the ragged cattails for so long have broken up and dispersed like crowds of sports fans.

Tiny warblers that navigated the night skies with the unerring direction of airliners have disappeared into the emerging leaves like the seeds of dreams.

Sandhill cranes that came pumping up from the south like the ghosts of pterodactyls now yodel from the remote corners of the wetlands, where they have established secret territories.

In short, millions of furred and feathered creatures have divided up the wild land with more neatness and harmony than suburban planners could ever hope for.

But the great spring search for places is not without its conflicts. A wood duck came one day to alight on the neighborhood squirrel nest, but the facility was not to her liking and she flew off toward the pond, perhaps to the relief of the squirrels. A sparrow checked out the hanging pottery gourd where the flying squirrels have been in residence for years; and a chipmunk made a brief exploration of the garage before dashing back under the deck.

And to mark its place, a flicker asserted its membership in the woodpecker family by hammering in the early morning on the bottom of the upended metal canoe in the back corner of the yard. It is a resonating sound, loud enough to wake the soundest sleeper.

Then there was the backyard cardinal crisis. The industrious pair of redbirds put their claim on a small hemlock tree and began to gather nest material. Of the half dozen hemlock, however, they chose the one that had died and was destined for early spring replacement. While there was still only a smattering of twigs assembled, the tree was removed to avert the greater disaster of a broken home involving youngsters. The cardinals were perplexed, to say the least, and fluttered aimlessly about for a couple of hours before moving into the neighbor's arbor vitae.

In the temporary gap left by the hemlock, you could look through the back yard and down a street, and see the couples that came to look at the vacant lot that is for sale there. They would stand on the edge of the street, pointing and talking, then they would get in their car and drive off, like the wood duck flying off from the squirrel nest or the chipmunk deciding against the garage.

In the midst of all of this, as the amber buds of maple did their popcorn impression and the willow trees got green with envy, the earth survived the hoopla of Earth Day, going about its age-old business with no more acknowledgment of the attention than a bleeding bull as the sword of the coup de grace is prepared.

So now, in the energy of the spring search, there is a dichotomy: The ills of the earth are disguised in vegetative finery and a frenzy of reproduction, but in that, the vulnerability is there, too, in the delicate nature of the very young of a thousand species, and in the fine, web-like connections that bind it all together.

Now, more than at any other time of the year, you can sense the fragility of it, like something whispering and spiritual that you can almost hear and almost feel. Almost, but not quite. And that is the pity.

EVERY MAN

The early morning mist, as worn and ragged as old lace, clung wraith-like to the field edges. The neighboring woods brushed at it with gnarled, green fingers, and before this gentle caress, tiny finches fluttered about like golden moths.

The field had been freshly plowed and planted, and when you stood beside it, the smell of raw earth filtered in through the pores of your being to make you feel like a seed.

In the rich pungency, there were the aromas of the ages, strange, unidentifiable odors, perhaps of wallowing dinosaurs and grinding glaciers. Then the cool mist along the edges became the hot steam of volcanic springs, or vapor rising from the great sheets of retreating ice. In such unbridled fantasizing, the high geologic drama that brought the soil of this field to this place became as real as the scream of the jay back in the woods, and those cataclysmic soil-making occurrences that in their combinations can hardly be imagined became as believable as the distant bellowing of a cow.

That this peaceful field—as still now in the morning as a grave—that this common, everyday field has a history more exciting than the wildest machinations of science fiction minds; and that its present state is no more permanent than its circumstance a million years ago; these facts were not so foreign now in the fresh light of this new day.

The field and everything around it was somehow stage-like, a set for the drama of the eons, where now a million silent earthworms supported the black earth in its stardom, and its eloquence was in its mute vitality. And in its damp glistening, pillowed by the mist and bedded between the soft new leaves, the soil had a sensuality that took in the universe.

Then against the deep shadows across the field, a man emerged from the gently writhing mist. He was dressed in dark green, and he stood very still and stared across the freshly planted field. He had materialized as quietly as the deer that had been there earlier to leave the deep hoofprints in the soft soil. And his appearance was as unobtrusive as the cottontail rabbit's when it came at dawn to eat the long stems of dandelions beneath the protection of the gray fog.

The man was alone, and there was no tractor or farm equipment in sight. Given that, his solitary presence had a mystical quality to it. Little effort was required, therefore, to transform him from flesh and blood into an ethereal representation of the ages. In his forest-green clothing and mist-washed countenance, he became the father and grandfather and uncle of us all. He was the quiet army of those men and women of the soil from whom we are all descended, some of us within generations and others within centuries. They march on in faded photo albums and museum exhibitions, and the great cities that developed with them and around them are nothing more than adjuncts to their efforts. As transmogrified as that relationship has become, its basic truth has not changed: Without the fields there could be no cities.

Across the expanse of black soil, the man in the morning mist was no man and every man, and his silence was one with the powerful, silent message of the soil. It said this: We are here now—the deer, the rabbit, the earthworms, the little golden birds, and you and I; and in the soothing quiet of this misty morning, we acknowledge the transient gift of this field from our great Mother Earth.

The man was gone then, back into the mist and the trees, and whether he was ever there might be a matter of conjecture, except for the footprints in the soft soil where he had been standing.

And then they, too, were gone.

This Is the Morning

It was a morning! It was a fine, fine thing that developed slowly out of the night rain, wearing soft gray fog and leading an exuberant choir of birds. It ignored the icy bones of winter decaying beneath the evergreen trees, and it advanced through the shadows with the authority of everything that has ever been and everything that will ever be.

The early spring morning was the simple mark of yet one more rotation of the earth, as taken for granted as the next breath; but in its muted character there was a womb-like quality to it, and out of it came the feeling of imminent universal rebirth.

This particular emergence of daylight commanded an extraordinary sensory focus: It brought a rare awareness that the moment is the essence of existence, and if this is not celebrated occasionally, then life turns in on itself and begins to shrivel.

The forlorn voices of geese, like hired mourners at the wrong gathering, came down out of the fog, crying in the imagination to fathoms of turbulent memory, of buried grief, of graves not yet settled and others not yet occupied.

And the wild, cackling laughter of the sandhill cranes rode over it all, their long, slim necks trumpeting from the swamps like the horns of Gabriel gone mad.

It was a morning of passage, a morning to give in to the relentless swing of time, to consort with the past only long enough to step beyond it. This is the morning. There have been others like it in the past, and there will be others like it in the future, but there is now only this morning, only this small block of time coming damp and gray out of the night and beckoning—no, *demanding* allegiance.

In the woods the heaviness of winter had pressed the carpet of leaves as flat as paper, and here and there the exposed runways of mice wound through the decaying debris. That the tiny creatures' chances for surviving the winter were proportionately equal to yours and mine is an undeniable truth that seemed to emanate from this singular morning with bemusement.

The spring pond was full to overflowing, and along its muddy banks, skunk cabbage poked up, the embryonic core of its cabbages protectively swaddled by the curl of its pointed, amber-colored leaves. In this distinctive morning of awakenings, it seemed only natural that the common old plant be recognized for evolving the capacity to produce its own heat to protect it from the spring frosts, and for its early start, so that it can develop those huge leaves that guarantee it a share of summer sun even beneath the smothering canopy of alder and dogwood.

Such adaptation is the key to nature's diversity, and now in the seasonal nakedness of the earth and the amiable freshness of this damp morning, it was logical to question your own modification to be a part of this otherwise harmonious scheme.

Crows argued. Squirrels scolded. A pair of woodcock zig-zagged up in flight plans of dementia. And far in the distance a barred owl called, the same old four-note inquiry, as if it had nothing new to say but simply wanted to participate in the morning.

Then the sun came slowly through the hazy mist and an arm of light reached down through the bare branches and illuminated the mosses and lichens, where the clear water bubbled up from the sand. It produced a wondrous blend of golden sunshine and the emerald green of lowly, tiny plant forms that cover the rotting logs and the rocks that sulk in the black muck. It was as if the morning had unveiled an unparalleled masterpiece there in the quiet woods, a work of such breathtaking creativity as to mock the blundering efforts of the finest artists.

It was there, and then the mist closed in and it was gone, except as it continued to exist in memory.

That alone is apparently the evolutionary gift we can bring to the special mornings: We can appreciate and remember their beauty, and thus equipped, we can recognize that to live them is to know that no one of them is better than the other, and they are all glorious.

THE COYOTE AND THE PIG

A solitary coyote trotted across a freshly planted field on a recent evening. It passed ghost-like through the twilight, at times fading into the brown earth colors to become invisible, then reappearing on the crest of the ridge, there to pause briefly and survey its surroundings.

The wild brother of dogs traveled the openness between farms, depending on the descending darkness to hide its activity and protect it from the curiosity and predation of civilization. It did not slink or sneak. It went forthrightly, using that portion of the circadian cycle that comes recommended to it by the eons.

The coyote's business and its destination were as private as the sealed orders of a spy, and there was such an aura of freedom and independence about the animal's phantom-like passage that it elicited a peculiar envy.

The coyote was visible from the busy interstate, where another animal passed by. It was a pig, and only its damp, pink snout could be seen through an opening in the side of a livestock truck that roared down the highway.

The pig was one of many confined in the truck, and they all rode to their doom behind the driver, who guided the ponderous vehicle toward the slaughterhouse with the unerring skill of a space navigator.

The pig's shiny snout caught the glint of passing headlights, and in its stoic protrusion out into the twilight, a pathos might be read, a sad story of domesticity's final betrayal.

So they went their ways on through the twilight and into the night, the coyote and the pig, and bits of the imagination went with them, parasitically, hanging on for the ride, like ticks.

And then in the morning, there were the two hammerings. They came in through the open bedroom window with volume enough to chase Morpheus, and it took a few seconds to sort them out.

First was the measured series of rat-a-tat-tats from the flicker that was using the upended metal canoe in the backyard as a resonator to announce its availability as a suitor, if not its domination over all other flickers within earshot. The woodpecker-type bird rapped at intervals of 20 seconds or so, stopping between raps to blink and look around for response. None was apparent, nor had any been apparent for the past three weeks of incessant hammering. But response is obviously only for the flicker to judge.

The other hammering came from the crew of roofers on the new house that has replaced the oak and hickory trees on a nearby lot. The roofers' hammering was not as measured as the flicker's, but it was louder, and there was a message of finality in its irregular beat. It said now this piece of land is forever taken over by a single species to the exclusion of all other species, except perhaps an occasional unwelcomed mouse, which will be forthwith dispatched by poison, traps, or professional exterminators.

The hammerings went on through the morning and at intervals all day long. By evening, the roofers had accomplished their job, and never again would a drop of rain fall on several thousand square feet of the good earth.

The flicker, meanwhile, had also finished for the day, and was nowhere to be seen as twilight shuffled in like a night-shift nanny. The bird's accomplishments, depending on perspective, were no less important than the new roof, and, of course, much less demanding on the natural community.

So in the lengthening shadows, you are left with that, and with a lingering curiosity about the current whereabouts of the coyote and the pig. Again in the grayness of this twilight, the coyote obviously roams free and wild somewhere across the brown fields.

The pig? The poor manipulated pig had no choice but to trade a few months of corn for a ride to the slaughterhouse. It is probably dead by now, on its way to becoming bacon for truck drivers and roofers and the other grand consumers of Earth's bounty.

Tomorrow, the morning will belong to the flicker, and the twilight to the coyote. Who can say what belongs to the pig, and to those of us who breakfast on bacon?

THE MORNING CHORUS

Sometimes there is such a flow of obdurate circumstances that the tightrope of life takes on a serpentine squirm and threatens to tumble the lot of us into a common hell. An ever-wondrous technology brings us gory details of the outrageous atrocities of our species until we are drunk with the awful knowledge, reeling, muttering, slinking. The senses begin to shut down, and we retreat from life like the possum, curling within ourselves and bracing for whatever comes: mauling dogs, boys with sticks, men with shovels.

But then, if we are lucky, the sweet music of life is suddenly there, and the creeping scalp is an old hat again, covering the brain that we cannot fathom in either its individual or collective machinations. Then from the depths, there is a keening of the spirit before Earth's majesty.

The music began in the folding black tent of night, in that circadian hush that preceeds the grand transition: A barred owl called from far back in the pine, its message at once one of summation and challenge.

And then, as if they wanted to start an argument, tom turkeys gobbled from high up in their shadowy roosts. Nobody knows why turkeys sass the owls in the first light of day. But they do, and it can be the turkeys' downfall when hunters prowl the woods. Given natural selection, the turkeys will probably cease and desist in a few thousand years, or maybe the hunters will cease before them, the final absurd antlers of a muley society.

The combination of hoots and gobbles resounds across the retreating darkness like a pre-concert riot in the brass section. It is loud but brief, and it has served tumultuous notice that it is time to get on with the day.

And as if it must read from the same sheet music, a sandhill crane yodels from a distant swamp, its crazy song rolling over the land like a pratfalling clown.

The light strengthens, and crows add their raucousness to the cacophony, their cawing like the plain voice of reason in the midst of madness.

Blue jays scream their claims to all that they survey, then fly off to hunt acorns where the skeletal oak stand in seasonal pregnancy.

From back by the pond, a mallard quacks with the authority of a first sergeant; then in the distance, geese talk to each other in that peculiar and familiar voice that is obviously faulty and would have been recalled if nature were subject to bureaucratic regulation.

The strange voices fill the morning, and in their blending there is the sweet music; and the listener is wrapped in and enraptured by the moment until the senses begin to open again, like the possum uncurling and opening its eyes, preparing to shuffle off into the uncertainty of life.

It goes on, fortissimo. Robins join in. Cardinals contribute their shrill whistling. A woodpecker volunteers something comparable to a kazoo. And at one point, a hawk glides overhead and shrieks down at the faintly greening earth.

So in this morning music, there is the signal of the great joining, the whistling and shrieking and bugling of the orchestra that is all of us and everything. Its reverberations are received beyond the depth of bone and marrow; and in the slow revival of the senses, there is the awesome question of appropriate morning sound for that occupant of evolution's highest rung.

Would that be a scream to greet the dawn—an explosive venting of vocal energy to express abject outrage at the species' incredible innate intransigence?

Would it be a moan to denote the ultimate sadness? Would it be a burst of callous laughter?

The wild sounds go on all around, building in intensity until the light of day is full and complete. Then they become more infrequent, as the creatures get on with the business of feeding and propagating.

The question of appropriate human participation is left unanswered. Somehow, it seems best to have appreciated it all in silence, listening to its healing symphonic qualities, then moseying off as restored as a resurrected possum.

GRADUATIONS

While most species are busy with the business of propagation during these asparagus days of spring, one species engages in a strange form of flocking: To borrow a phrase from the late, lamented Pogo, "It is us."

Now in May and on into June, we flock together in a great variety of joyous rituals that seem to make very little sense in the natural scheme of things.

Many of the gatherings have to do with graduations, those occasions that mark a youthful clan member's completion of a prescribed course of formal training. The generations assemble, bearing modest gifts and boundless pride, and at no other time do the perspectives of different ages meld into such a pleasant spectrum of sensation and emotion. The graduate is breathless with his or her own possibilities and potential. Parents are choked up with a job well-done—perhaps, at given moments, even perfectly done. And the older members, grandparents and aunts and uncles, smile and see shadows of themselves; then a sense of mortality gives them a little kiss on the ear.

But overall, these rites are characterized by such exuberance and happiness as to be contagious, and the spirit of spring effervesces out to everyone.

The earliest version of this seasonal ceremony was probably enacted by thick-browed ancestors, when they gave grunting approval to an offspring who was quick to learn how to collect bird eggs.

It has come down to us to include caps and gowns and flowering speeches, and in some respects it just might mark the highest scratch we have been able to make on the evolutionary tree.

But it may not be unique to us. Other species know similar kinds of flocking, and these too correlate to the young having reached a certain stage of independence. Most of them are in the fall, and they are as common as swirling flocks of blackbirds or gabbling hordes of geese.

A spectacular example occurs when the sandhill cranes gather from hundreds of miles around. It is a breathtaking thing to see, hundreds of the huge birds standing about in clusters and groups, filling the air with their cries and appearing to have no other purpose but getting together to mark the arrival of a generation. You cannot witness it without sensing, in its collective energy and restless spirit, a special kind of wild celebration.

It is unquestionably a graduation, and certainly in the cranes' yodeling you can hear a version of "Pomp and Circumstance."

Then, slowly, with what seems to be deliberate disorder, the birds rise singly and in small groups, to catch thermals and disappear over the horizon.

This isn't all that much different from our graduations, except that we hold ours in the spring.

Summer

River Voices

The clear, cool water that still flows in wild rivers is the clean blood of history, and now in the summer you can hear voices there, old voices, sometimes whispering in the slicks and eddies, sometimes shouting in the rocky, roaring rapids.

Sometimes the voices are so distinct they make you stop and listen. There is no one there, of course, or is there?

There is a place where cedar trees brush the rushing water with dark boughs, and great boulders defy the power of the rapids. A small jut of flat land lies at the foot of the rapids, and still discernible beneath the thick trees is the outline of a structure, its dimensions set by the decaying logs that formed its sides.

It was used a century ago by the lumberjacks who cut the great trees and then tended the spring log drives to float the wild land's first crop to a consuming civilization.

Part way up the rapids, a huge gray stump sits solidly on the rocky riverbank. Its sides are gouged by ax marks, made long ago when it might have been used as a fulcrum to help break up the logjams that were terrifying in their power and capriciousness. Or perhaps it held a rope that a calk-booted man clung to as he tried to maneuver the ponderous logs, a futile lifeline of sorts in a business and time that would trade a man's life for a log in a minute, and often did. A brief scream in the grinding crunch of logs and thundering water. No body. No funeral. Just a wooden stake beside the river to mark the spot.

The stump is there like a monument to that time of brave and foolish young men, and to long-suffering women who waited in vain for them to come home in the summer. It is a decaying altar, where you can pay homage to a brief and passionate page of history.

You cannot come to the stump or the rapids without hearing the voices. There are mumbling conversations of loves and dreams, businesslike commands to accomplish the work of the day, and shouts to horses and companions. Then suddenly, for no apparent reason, there is a scream, or is there? Was it just the summer wind, or the twist of a branch against the hissing water?

Now we come to the wild country to play—to canoe and fish—and the rushing stream puts us in our place. A hundred years from now, no one will ever know we were here, unless our whoops of fun are somehow added to the summer voices of the river.

The Bullet Lady

It was the summer that the sideshow lady caught a bullet in her teeth.

You don't get many summers like that in a lifetime, maybe only two or three. They come when the music of life is being played on magnificent strings and crashing cymbals, when the senses are in a joyous stampede to reach destinations of forbidden mystery, after Santa Claus and the tooth fairy and before pimples.

The summers then are the sweetest slices from the cake of time, and we gobble them down like the children that we are, unaware until much later of their rare quality.

We consumed that summer as the current one is being consumed by a similar age group, that wide-eyed crowd of freckles, sunburn, and bicycle bruises.

That particular summer was on the land like a great, green robe. All things simmered within it: Plants thrived, animals loafed, birds perched with beaks agape, and human emotions sometimes flared. You heard rumors, even as a child. A neighbor was in jail for fighting. A woman disappeared, leaving a baffled family behind.

But mostly, the summer was a cascade of sun-drenched days, each one like a present, wrapped in dew and delight.

Then there was the county fair, and the days emerged from summer lethargy like a boar coming out of a mud wallow. The air was suddenly laden with rich smells: animal odors, popcorn, caramel candy. A kaleidoscope of crazy color replaced the summer green, and a fine dust rose up to become a haze that made it seem as if nothing was real.

The bullet lady was in a big canvas tent, next to the

twisted little man who sat in a small enclosure full of snakes. She wore a long, slinky dress that was missing a few sequins, and she stood behind a podium with a small piece of glass in front of her.

The build-up of suspense in the shadowy tent was enough to threaten a boy's bladder control, and when the shot finally came, it was even more sorely tested. The explosion of the gun filled the tent like a storm, the glass shattered, and the lady in the slinky dress made a face and spit a bullet into a round metal pie plate, which was then passed in front of the audience as proof of the feat.

Other things were to go on in the tent, but they were only for adults, so the adolescent consumers of summer were shooed outside, where they stood blinking in the bright sunlight, looking at each other and never doubting for a second that they had gotten their money's worth, even though the show was not yet over.

Lord, Lord, but that was a summer!

THE STRANGER

It was one of those flawless summer days: pillow clouds, golden sun, the air laden with that dichotomous blend of energy and lethargy, when young things grow like weeds and progenitors dare to breathe deeply.

Half-grown sparrows chirped incessantly from a nest somewhere nearby, and the muted sounds of a small town played like an orchestra tuning up far in the distance.

The little girl, delicate and waiflike, her brown hair arranged in scraggly wisps by morning play and the summer breeze, wandered over from the park, where she had been playing with a trio of friends.

She stood before me and watched as I leaned against the back of the car and plunked on an old banjo while waiting for my wife, a practice that would have made me another Earl Scruggs long ago except for a dearth of talent.

The little girl looked at the banjo and then at me.

I smiled at her, obviously in violation of current wisdom about how to help protect children from the perverts and monsters among us.

She looked me in the eye then, and said, "Are you dangerous?"

It was such a ridiculous question, asked in such glorious innocence, that it was all wonderful and frightening at the same time. How do you respond to such a thing in a way that demonstrates to a child the inherent compassion of the human spirit but also warns of its aberrations?

Her little friends had joined her and one of them, a tow-headed boy with skinned knees, said, "You're a stranger, aren't you?"

The questions were piling up.

"No," I said, "I am not dangerous, and yes, I am a stranger."

And I felt obligated to add that some strangers were dangerous.

The kids nodded solemnly and said there had been another stranger in the park earlier, wearing a blue shirt, and he drove away in a black car.

They lost interest in me then, or perhaps my banjo drove them away. They plodded off down the sidewalk, full of the serious business of being children on a beautiful summer day.

The little girl turned and gave me one last look. I smiled at her again. I couldn't help it: Her wispy, childish beauty and her innocence had filled me with a mingled sense of great sadness and boundless joy.

Then I was alone, a stranger amid the chirping of sparrows.

INNER STORMS

The summer rains rinse the starch out of our spines now and leave us limp-spirited.

At the least, picnic plans are canceled, and we are disappointed. At the most, floods force us from our homes and leave us in sodden misery.

The rain reminds us that before the elements we are as insignificant as specks of dust, no more in control of our destinies than are feathers in the wind.

Sometimes the rain sneaks in unannounced, like the ghost of a prior storm. One moment it is not here, then it begins to sift down out of the gray overcast to touch your face with its cold-lipped kiss.

Other times, the rain comes sloshing in like a conquering armada. It is as if an endless stream of clouds collapses overhead, and their liquid burdens descend like waterfalls. Then it seems impossible that some basic law of physics has not been violated: How could so much water, considering its weight and volume, defy gravity long enough to fall at this time and at this place?

There is something ominous about it. Perhaps it touches something deep within us, some ancient genetic history that has to do with our slither out of the watery mire.

The summer rains that are packaged in thunderstorms also pluck the strings of our psyche until it twangs like a banjo. Thunderheads, towering castles of godlike whim, build in the west, and as they tumble toward us they push clouds as black as night into our day. We scurry then, along with the birds and the creatures, to seek shelter. Children are rounded up and herded inside. Windows are closed as the explosive cracks of thunder jar us to the marrow, and the first gusts of wind sweep in like the broom of an angry Almighty.

Then it is all there at once: booming thunder, flashing lightning, buffeting wind, and sheets of rain, sometimes mixed with pellets of ice.

There are explanations for all of it: hot air and cold air, positive and negative charges, convection and precipitation. But caught in the middle of it, the mind chooses not to sort through this kind of calm logic. Instead, it reacts to the sensory input it receives, and the storm becomes as personally threatening as an attacker who would reduce you to whimpering and trembling, like something that might have cowered in a dark cave eons ago.

It was a cruel schoolboy trick, in which I claim only brief participation, but sometimes we would pour buckets of water down a gopher burrow until the drenched creature was forced to scurry out another hole. Sometimes the rain makes us feel as those gophers must have felt: threatened, desperate, ready to brave the worst of dangers to escape the water that pours down into every crack and cranny of life.

We have only one small advantage over the gopher: We know that eventually the rain will stop, and the sun will shine. Sometimes, however, that simple knowledge is too sodden to recall.

THE AWESOME DEMOCRACY

Suddenly the earth is as extravagant as first love, bursting at its green seams with undisciplined growth and sorting through its own lushness for the exquisite harmony. It is a time to celebrate inclusion in the majesty of it all, and to embrace your own species for some nebulous reassurance of your personal existence.

So we traveled north to the hard, wild country of Ontario, where the granite bedrock comes up like the exposed bones of the planet, and for a few days we severed the technologic umbilical cord that threatens to turn us all into soft, staring zombies.

Certainly they were grandsons in the literal sense of the word—Andy, 9, and Steve, 8—and the fact that their father had to stay home and they were "forced" to miss the last week of school, made our alliance an escape of good proportions. We shared, in fact, the general mood of successful cookie thieves as we drove across the border and joined the family males at the fishing camp.

Then we were back on the wilderness lake, accessible only by boat or float plane, living in tents and keeping a campfire going and more or less wallowing in the hours and the days. No job, no school, nobody to get overly concerned about matters of grooming and diet. And no television!

We caught jagged-toothed northern pike, barracuda-like fighters that came scowling into the boat ready to brawl with the world, and at times the excitement level made the loons yodel like cheerleaders. We released the fish because, well, after talking it over, it seemed like the right thing to do, and the other fishermen were catching plenty of them for eating.

We explored hidden rivers and waterfalls, and a cliff where someone—perhaps an early Indian—had painted geometric figures. We picked up beaver-chewed sticks and poles and watched the seagulls fight over the fish guts back at camp. And sometimes we just sat around the campfire and stared into it until the smoke made us move, which it always did.

Separated as we were by two generations, we fell into a comradeship that de-emphasized authority and put a priority on individual choice. We were a democracy in its purest sense—one boy (or man), one vote—though as a practical matter, one of us had veto power.

One afternoon, when the parade of white clouds was like a pillow fight among the gods, we took a lunch and boated to a big rounded mass of granite, where huge boulders perched as if waiting for someone to give them a push. We used one of the rocks for a table, and ignored the black flies as best we could as we ate a lunch of cheese and sausage and apples. Then we explored the moss and lichen, and Steve found a big brown eggshell that we puzzled over.

One of the boulders—so big the boys could just see over it—seemed to have an especially precarious perch. Then, when a smaller stone was kicked away, the ponderous boulder went bounding down the granite, knocking down a big dead tree and plunging into the lake with a mighty splash.

In the quiet that followed, Andy stared after the boulder and said, "Awesome!"

One afternoon a cow moose and her calf entertained us briefly as they went lumbering up the hillside and disappeared into the trees, and on another occasion, a beaver slapped the water close by and startled us.

One night, the northern lights came shooting and streaking overhead, in a spectacular invasion of silent beams and flares. Another time, the full moon balanced on the sharp tips of the black spruce and threatened to roll right into camp for a game of orange ball.

Taken as a whole, the adventure was just one of those silly, ritualistic exercises that are endemic and epidemic now in this warm season. It was just some males doing one of their foolish tribal things, and there was nothing any more sexist about it than the way boys sometimes use their special equipment to write their names in the snow.

It was all pretty well wrapped up in Andy's one-word assessment of the boulder incident: In terms of escape, enjoyment, production of memories and species as well as personal reassurance, it was indeed "Awesome!"

THE BRICK WALL

This summer has been hot and dry enough to kill love. Maybe that's why that old summer comes back so vividly, like someone dear and gone smiling through the golden haze. It was the summer of Geraldine, a budding little lovely who captured my boyish heart with her soft hints of a mysterious and tantalizing world beyond puberty.

Then Geraldine and my love were carried away by a horse, my horse, and that summer is stamped indelibly in my mind, like a scribbled crayon picture that might have become a Van Gogh, except for equestrian betrayal. Never again would I feel the same about Geraldine, or my horse, or summer.

The horse was actually a pony. His name was Silver, and he had carried me—always on his terms—through the cowboy days of boyhood, when rescuing ranchers' daughters was no more biologically entwined than collecting rocks.

Silver decided early on that he would never go more than a quarter of a mile from home. I would ride him to the quarter-mile mark, and he would stop as if a brick wall blocked his path.

The secret of mastering a horse, of course, is in using your larger brain to offset the horse's larger brawn. I wasn't up to it, and after a struggle at the "brick wall," during which I alternated between pleas and tears, Silver would decide he had had enough and head for home. Sometimes he would buck me off first, and sometimes he would let me ride along.

A child who has a pony is considered lucky, even indulged, but it wasn't that way with Silver. I think my father bought the pony to teach me how contrary and impossible the world can be.

Finally, however, the occasion arose when it seemed that Silver's geographic stubbornness would pay off for me. Geraldine, who was visiting my sister, decided she wanted to ride Silver up the road to a neighboring farm to see a couple of older boys.

I cooperated in this, catching Silver and wrestling on the bridle and saddle, because I knew Silver would stop at the brick wall. Then he'd turn and bring Geraldine back to me, whereupon she would recognize how fortunate she was to be in my company.

But it didn't happen that way. For the first time in his life, the rotten little pink-nosed pony went past the brick wall as if it weren't there. The last thing I saw was Geraldine's curls, tossing in the breeze as Silver carried her to more worldly and interesting males.

Geraldine, with the conspiratorial help of my own pony, broke my heart that day, and when I tried to tell myself it didn't matter, the message didn't take. Somehow, I couldn't go back to the imaginary ranchers' daughters: They seemed to have lost their substance and now were boring, even silly.

So now I grieve again for the innocence of childhood that began to break down on that hot, dry summer day long ago. It's an exercise I must suffer annually, and in its throes I try to remember that out of it came the resolve needed to make Silver go through the brick wall the next time I rode him. Of course, he bucked me off and ran home shortly thereafter.

THE UNINVITED GUEST

The other creatures worry when I come to the stream on a summer evening. Their voices are whispered complaints in the rising steam of the cooling day: hisses, squawks, squeaks, snorts.

What, they ask, is this clumsy, clumping critter doing in our pristine parlor? He has no business here, him with his absurd little fishing wand and the odd trinkets hung from his vest. We get along so well without him, why doesn't he stay on the concrete where he belongs?

He is here to rob our nests, charge the blackbirds, wheeling overhead and scolding frantically. Just when the young are hatching and it is such a worrisome time, we do not need his kind stumbling about in the reeds like a moose!

He is here to chase me and my young family up and down the stream, claims the mallard hen. He has the look of a predator, but seems to lack the cunning. Would he eat duckling? Probably. We must flee his awkward bumbling.

From the oak trees, the whippoorwill's yipping call bounces off the hillside and mimics the sound of the fly-rod whipping through the air. A rank amateur at whipping sounds, says the whippoorwill—a dolt, if the truth be known. He should be banned from the valley for fraudulent whipping.

He claims to be a wader, says the heron, sailing through the twilight on silent wings. Look at him staggering through the mud like a cow. He wades as if he wore leg-irons of nettles. I could teach him a thing or two, but it would be hopeless.

Obviously he has come to interfere with my salad

course, says the muskrat. I should dive down and bite a hole in his waders. But he would only patch them and come back: He is too thick-skulled to understand the message in such gestures.

He will probably step on my nest when he finally walks out across the pasture, laments the killdeer. There is no more sensitivity in his feet than if they were stones. But he's a sucker for the broken-wing trick. It works every time, and him claiming to be so smart.

Look at him swing that ridiculous gossamer line with the phony insect made of feathers, says the cedar waxwing. He knows nothing of insects, not even enough to fool the stupid fish—or is he casting for birds, since his pitiful imitation fly spends more time in the air than on the water?

Beware of that wildly swinging line, says the bat, lest it snare you around the neck. It happened to a relative of mine. Caught fast, it was pulled off the rod with such force that it smacked him in the back of the neck, and he hooted like an owl.

So, says the doe from the darkness of the ridge. It is all of this and more that offends me, and if he were smart enough to translate my sneezing snorts, he could never be more insulted.

Sometimes along the stream, I feel the loneliness from all of those speeches, and I know then that there is no way for the uninvited guest to ingratiate himself. He must sneak away, and come back only when his unmanageable arrogance reasserts itself.

GRANDFATHER'S WALTZ

In the sweet music of summer, Grandfather Helgeland's walk was a one-man waltz, his body dipping with each step and his arms swinging like pendulums. I see him now in the hayfield, the sun sucking still more of the blue from his faded shirt and turning the back of his neck to dry leather.

He was a thin, gangly man with a sharp nose and friendly blue eyes that to me as a boy were like small portholes offering glimpses of mysterious places and times. The trick was to look into them, because they were rarely still enough for anything but a glance. The eyes were as busy as the rest of Grandfather.

The image of him comes clearly now as the heat of the sun turns the upper Midwest into a giant batch of green popcorn and the stewards of the land must do their sweaty summer dances. It was in the summer that I came to visit, fluttering about him like a moth and getting in his way.

Before the days of choppers and balers, putting up a winter's supply of hay was a tedious, back-breaking summer task, and Grandfather bent to it like an ant moving a sandwich. Pitchfork in hand, he wrestled with towering mounds of hay until he was sweat-drenched and gasping for breath. He was at war with time and circumstance, hopelessly disadvantaged except that he kept up the struggle and eventually won. The barn was full of hay. My skinny grandfather had performed some kind of strange miracle, gathering up the skin of the earth like tissue paper and cramming it neatly into storage. Sometimes I would climb into the haymow to lie in its prickly pungency and try to comprehend the significance of Grandfather's accomplishment.

Granddad's Scandinavian skin was thin and easily torn, and sometimes blood would run from the backs of his hands in tiny ruby rivers. He would pay no attention, never even pausing to wipe it away with the big red handkerchief he carried in a hip pocket. I was amazed by that, incredulous and speechless before a man who was too busy to bleed to death.

One summer, leopard frogs were in the grain stubble like an invasion from a planet of amphibians. They made great, flying leaps ahead of Grandfather as he grabbed up the bundles of grain and built shocks that to me were little thatch-roofed houses. Once I hid in one of them and became the commander of the frogs, and when Grandfather heard me issuing orders, I saw him smile. He didn't pause, but he smiled, and I saw something in his blue porthole eyes that made me feel good.

Grandfather wore out about the time I got old enough to do anything but get in his way. It happened suddenly. One day he was swinging along in his waltzing gait, and the next he was lying flat in bed and couldn't feed himself. He didn't last long that way: The burden of immobility crushed the life from him as certainly as if he had been executed.

Many summers have passed since he was laid to rest in a country cemetery. But on a recent summer day, I saw Grandfather's walk again. It was performed by my brother, who did not know I was watching him. The swaying dip between steps was there, and the arm swinging; something about it made me feel good, like the time Grandfather smiled at me as I talked to the frogs.

THE COMMON POOL

Rain is life to flowers and trees . . . and to that boy or girl who stands watching us all from way back in the metamorphic shadows.

The first raindrops splattered on the metal shed roof like bullets. The sound built then to a thunderous drum roll, and a shimmering curtain of silvery white came down across the front of the open door.

A quartet of barn swallows perched on a wooden beam like glum little judges, twittering occasional objections at their confinement and preening at their perfect feather robes.

Along the back wall, where the dirt floor stayed cool even on the hottest summer days, a wise old dog lay curled in dreams, twitching now and then and emitting an occasional grunt at the height of somnolent chases.

The shed was a private puttering place for the boy, a refuge of tools and things where thought and actions could fly like the swallows or get lost in dreams like the dog. The rain came to the boy like a spectral voice, speaking in tongues of things never spoken, of thoughts and feelings, stirrings and fears, all balanced on the treacherous edge of adulthood's abyss.

All summer, the sun had burned down out of a cloudless sky, turning the boy as brown as dirt and baking cracks of worry into his father's brow. A pall had descended to wilt the joyous bouquet of summer, and the boy had felt it in his being, like a faint nausea from too many green apples or the sadness of a disappointing truth. It had colored his play, making it dry and gritty; it had interfered with his chores, adding stifling heat to the burdens in the buckets of water and animal feed.

The dryness had been everywhere, licking up the sparse morning dew before the sun was up and filling the mouth of night with black cotton, so that it moaned for a drink. The dryness sat at the kitchen table and mocked the conversation there, demanding attention above all things, and getting it.

Sometimes in the afternoon, thunderheads built in the west—bulging, towering things that seemed too large to be of this world. They would roll overhead in a great, pillowy parade and only once did they deliver so much as a drop of rain. Then it had been like spit, an insult from sadistic gods, and the boy had taken it personally.

But then the rain came, suddenly it seemed, out of a sky that turned from blue to gray without fanfare. No thunder or lightning. No sweeping wind to make the trees bow. Just rain, coming straight down in a torrent that went on and on.

The boy watched it from the shelter of the shed, then he stepped into it to feel the sudden chill and then the soothing caress of it on his brown body. He spread his arms and raised his face to the rain, shutting his eyes and opening his mouth to taste its clean flavor. Then he was something other than a boy, and he felt himself slip toward the edge of a great, common pool that he did not understand.

And in the downpour, a memory was germinated.

THE TRAFFIC TOLL

Now in the cornucopia of summer, the roads and highways are strewn with a million corpses, bloodied, battered, and flattened. Once they were the fluttering, shuffling, trotting, leaping, slithering life forms that the season produces with such bounty, then they were the unsightly remains that litter the roadways.

We, of course, are the architects of that negative transition. We do it with shiny, hurtling machines that hiss along the "game trails" like high-speed bulldozers, oblivious to all but the largest creatures and destroying even those.

Gophers stand along the roadsides now like funny little traffic cops, their backs as straight as sticks and their scampers across the traffic lanes often fatal.

Half-grown rabbits never make it to adulthood as they decide the grass is greener on the other side of the road; and millions of birds die as they slam against glass and metal in innocent flights from one bush to the next.

Deer, of course, are everywhere; their darting movement is totally unpredictable, and threatening to all drivers who do not drive slow enough to handle any possibility.

The gray squirrel was in the middle of the road when it sensed the car's approach. It headed down the centerline, doing a zig-zag run that has obviously come down the genetic pipeline to save it from stooping hawks and owls. But it doesn't work with vehicular traffic. The back and forth run only confuses the driver, and the squirrel's only hope is that the driver slows enough to permit the playing out of the zig-zag retreat.

The seagull was in the convenience store, standing in

an aisle with one wing drooping to the floor. It had been found on a customer's automobile grille, and the store clerk had agreed to take the bird until professional humane help could be called. The gull stood with quiet dignity near the beer cooler, and the great questions loomed over it like the worst storm it had ever experienced: How could a gull fly with only one wing, and not flying, how could it survive? Furthermore, without its effortless, graceful flight, would it *want* to survive?

The raccoon's carcass was just on the edge of the grass-line at the shoulder of the road, and the wind blew its tail in a strange, methodic cadence. But there was no wind! The injured raccoon was doing an unconscious march into oblivion, too crippled to do anything but move its tail and one leg that dug into the sand to make the same scratching track over and over and over.

Then, on a country road through wooded hills, a bull snake crawled out to soak the heat of the asphalt up through its belly. It was there in the middle of the road when the car rounded the bend, just a short distance away. Obviously, it sensed the onrushing torrent of movement in its flicking tongue, but it could not escape, nor could the driver avoid its sudden slithering. A tire ran over the snake's head and it twisted into a contorted mass.

The snake straightened itself out then, and in a bizarre reflex, thrust its body straight up, so that two or more feet of its five-foot length rose over the road, then fell back down. It went that way into the roadside weeds, the skyward thrust of its death dance movement an awful reptilian objection to its fate.

The weeds closed around the snake: blue chicory, white Queen Anne's lace, yellow goldenrod. It is an endless, magnificent funeral bouquet that waves everywhere now over the mutilated corpses and the dying creatures.

OLD DROUGHTS

The hot wind moves across the land now, like a draft from hell. It sucks the moisture from the soil until it hardens and cracks, and it licks at the vegetation with a million dry tongues until the grass turns brown and the leaves wither and quake.

Perhaps by the time you read this, the rains will have come, but now there is a drought that reaches into the heart of all things. Several weeks ago, when it was only days old, it reached into the heart of metropolitan Chicago, where commodity traders play poker with seeds. That means, of course, that you and I will pay for this drought at the grocery store, no matter its duration.

Now there is a hoarding of moisture across the land. Now, when the cellular program calls for explosive growth, plants of all descriptions have turned down their metabolism to "idle," and they wait, curled inward on themselves in a kind of biologic cowering.

That must be the posture now in the seasonal torture, to cower and conserve, and to reflect on the importance of moisture to our lives. For years, we take it for granted, even curse it when it descends in torrents and floods our basements, and then one day we look at the sky uneasily and realize that something is wrong: A metallic haze rims the cloudless horizon, and it comes as something of a shock to realize that there has been no rain for a long, long time.

But technology has built us a shelter from the drought. It is constructed of tanks and pumps and pipes and faucets, and we turn to it as automatically as we would scratch an itch. Water flows to our command, and we use this means to become little gods, to help some of the plants, the grass that we want green, and the flowers that we want to blossom.

However, we can only do so much, and it is really only a cosmetic little token, like pinning one medal on an army. The magnitude of a drought cannot be stemmed, not even when the technology extends to endless fields where irrigation systems sweep with great watery brooms.

In the city, the drought is an inconvenience. In the country, it is devastation, and those who live there know the feeling of despair that comes to the senses like tiny particles of gritty dust.

One summer, when arid, rainless days piled up one after another like hot-air balloons, the rural community where I lived as a boy began to curl up at the edges like a potato chip. Farmers, my father among them, had survived the Dust Bowl days as young men, and a decade later, as the drought moved in to cripple their crops with its hot, poisonous breath, there was a mixture of incredulity and fear among them. They would stand alone or with neighbors on the ends of the fields, staring off across the dryness and the brittle remains of their crops, and in their silence there was an expression of grand agony, something beyond pleading and whimpering.

Along the country roads, dust lay thick enough to cover the toes of a barefoot boy, and the passage of cars and trucks was marked by tornado-like clouds that swirled and spiraled up and rode off with the wind like ghosts rising from the dying land.

Pastures turned brown, and it was a cruel irony for farm boys assigned to thistle-cutting that the thistles with their long taproots seemed to flourish as the grass died around them.

The rains came, finally, as they always do. But the drought left a scar on the economy of the community, threatening to topple it back into the throes of the recent depression. Bank loans were extended and increased, and the fallout lasted until the next season, when there was no shortage of rain.

Droughts leave scars on people, too. Somewhere in the psyche of many of us is the mark of the post-Dust Bowl drought. That may be why now, as the current drought holds sway, we sometimes wake from a sound sleep to hear something peculiar and woeful in the night wind.

THE WILD SOUNDS

We slip back toward the water during the hot, steamy days of August. We go there to cool off, but we are also tugged along mysteriously by the ragged threads of the evolutionary umbilical cord, and we hear strange sounds from our muddy past.

The sounds come to us like the trumpets of lesser Gabriels, like the squawks of things long gone, and our ears are somehow awkward and inept before them.

Bass Lake, rimmed with jewel-like water lilies and tiny tufts of cotton sedge, produces some of these strange sounds. The small lake lies beautiful and shiny in the wilderness, like a stolen hand-mirror of the queen that has been cast away amid the rocks and trees.

At night around the lake, giant bullfrogs as big as rat terriers belch their bass love song. Its tuba-like resonance sets off sympathetic vibrations in your bones, and they undulate and quiver in old dances from other ages.

Early in the morning, when mist is on the lake like a negligee, the crazy, laughing call of the loon is suddenly everywhere, an eruption of madness in a cathedral of quiet.

This sound, too, probes deep, but more in inquisition than exposition, and the vague question it poses is this: Can there be a natural rhythm and reason to it all, or are we part of a great joke, in which cells are clustered to become ridiculous things—frogs, loons, humans?

One afternoon, when a summer breeze had seeded the lake with sun diamonds and bluegills were kissing bugs off the lily pads, a plaintive, bleating sound came sliding across the bay. It was at once strong and insistent, yet underlain with a note of desperation. A fawn had obviously been separated from its mother, and it bawled in the universal language of dependent young.

This sound probed to another depth, one less psychic and more biologic. There was a temptation to interfere, to go see if the fawn's distress was more than parental separation, perhaps a hunting coyote or a marauding dog. But then the bleating stopped, and so the temptation died aborning.

Then in the night again there were the bullfrogs, and they were joined briefly by a barred owl. The bird's call has been anthropomorphized to become an inquiry as to our identity: "Who, Who, Who?"

Who, indeed. There can be no certain answer for the owl, or for ourselves. As we haunt watery places in the heat of the summer, the wondrous sounds of the wild ridicule the conviction that we have risen to a point where we are no longer a part of the natural scheme.

So sometimes if we slither in doubt, it is a fitting summer exercise.

THE FALLEN APPLE

In the stillness of a hot afternoon, one small, green crab apple lost its grip and plummeted downward, whispering apologies to the leaves that it touched and landing with a thump as soft as a heartbeat. In its brief plunge, the apple had carried its tiny white-worm passengers from the airiness of the summer sky, where birds were in concert, to the musty closeness of the weed-covered earth, where a thousand insects worked decomposition claims.

The apple fell in the loneliness of a long-abandoned farmstead, where only the crumbling remains of a stone foundation and a few warped boards from the twisted corner of a shed hinted of a peopled past.

But in the faint stirring of the afternoon and in the apple's premature descent, the hints grew like August corn, and the people stepped out to soft, hissing cues.

The first were youthful and full of hope. They grubbed out stumps and set out the apple tree and planted the lilacs out by the road, and in the turning of the virgin soil, they were the progenitors of honest ambition in a land of brawling opportunists. And if they were cultural innocents, they were as true to themselves as cats, and they slept the sleep of the righteous. They were, in a way, the mothers and fathers of us all, pioneers of our spirits, searching for something better and for continuity, and we owe them our souls.

In the humidity of the afternoon near the apple tree, there is a sense of old sweat, of hard-muscled bodies caught in the past and shackled like prisoners to the trudging dumbness of horses, or locked to the stubborn inertia of hand tools.

The vulnerability of these intrepid people, their dependence on benevolent elements, is even now advertised in the billboard thunderheads that loom off to the south; and remnants of their despair from devastating hail or crushing wind must linger like gray bats in the rotting boards of the last outbuilding.

In the gentle breeze that caresses the crumbling foundation where the small house once stood, the sighs of their love-making are suspended in time like the whispers of butterfly wings.

Those moments translate to the shouts and laughter of children, who were once here as certainly as the crickets that now hide in the roots of the lilacs. The haunting sounds of their playing are in the shrieks and whimpers of the blue jays and the whistling of the cardinals.

Once the crab apples surely came to the late summer as pure as dew, no worms and no blemishes. And then the threshing crew ate them like grapes, and the children had apple fights that raised welts on their sun-browned skin. And the apples went into dozens of canning jars that were lined up on cool basement shelves, storing the sweet taste of summer for bland winter days.

In the slight freshening of the afternoon breeze, the apple tree stirs and a melancholia descends, perhaps the ghostly fruit of trouble that visited here. Sometimes in these places, the spirit was crushed like a clod of sterile soil. A child died. Love died. Ambition died. Dreams died. First the brightness of beginnings, then the dimness of endings. Like apples: from blossoms to fruit to brief fermenting to mold.

What happened here? Where are those sweaty stewards of the soil, those brave gamblers who drew against God Himself, those sighing lovers, those children who played here, and those men and women whose hearts were once planted here like seeds?

Gone, gone, gone.

All gone, except for those who came back for this reunion on the occasion of gravity, summoning one wormy, green crab apple.

From the Valley of Sleep

Questions for the end of a summer night, when the release from sleep means that life goes on, an occasion of such subtle personal celebration as to disguise itself in reluctance:

Where did we go last night, when consciousness flew off like a flock of satiated bats?

Where is that place of timelessness and darkness that we enter through the mysterious portals of sleep?

How do we explain the circadian metamorphose of dreams issuing like butterflies from the inert larvae that slumber makes of us?

Something shuffled across the roof while the darkness still prevailed, something going through the tail end of night with purposeful, scratching footsteps: A raccoon to sleep away the day in a chimney flue? A squirrel eager to get to the front-yard hickory tree and its extravagant crop of nuts? The troll-like keeper of dreams gathering up remnants for recycling?

Even then it starts, in the very first stages of awakening, when the senses are too muddied to deal with the eternal flow of uncertainties. Then, even as embryo, the day begins its teasing of the intellect, its baiting of the ego, its demands for analysis and assessment. But the only safe call is that the earth continues to spin, setting the cycles and recruiting the allegiance of every finite particle with its eternal whirling. Everything else is subject to the whims of the natural community and to the absurdity of interpretation.

One morning a storm came with the daylight, cracking its lightning whips against the windows and stomping its thundering feet through the backyards. The rain beat down out of the tumultuous wind in a noisy cascade, as if it celebrated escape; and in the elemental turbulence of it, there was a sense that something beyond comprehension was loose on the land, perhaps some force from the bottomless mystery of sleep, a marauding nightmare somehow out of its medium and out of control.

Rain swept over the big oak in back of the house in green quivering spasms, rinsing the night shadows out of the tree's serrated leaves and accentuating the creases in its alligator hide. Before the buffeting of the storm, the oak became a dark, dancing thing, wild and bowing, possessed suddenly with strange rudimentary energy, like an entity from the netherworld of tenebrous dreams.

Had there been some mysterious collapse of physiological barriers? Was it simply the ravages of an early morning storm sweeping over the neighborhood in that transitory time of awakening, or had something escaped from the darkness we enter each night as alone as feral cats? Was there to be now in consciousness the impotence of sleep, when there is no control and the raging of the alien and the bizarre assaults us until we cry and whine in our insensibility like blind kittens?

This thing—this electrical storm that might have been a fugitive force from somnolence—moved off toward the east with thunderous growling. Its echoes died like the snarling and barking of great hounds in hot pursuit of something huge and tormented. Then it was gone, leaving in its wake a swirl of gray mist and the drip, drip, drip of water bleeding back into the earth to the cardiac pull of gravity.

In the lifting of the grayness, birds left their cowering and claimed the morning. They came out of the shadows like the flotsam and jetsam of the storm, to twitter and flutter and preen.

There was nothing to do but join them, to engage the storm-washed summer day and hope that it had only been a slumber-induced illusion that something had crossed over from the valley of sleep, and we might now actually have to live with our outrageous nightmares and our ludicrous dreams.

THE MAW

The night wind is full of gossip, hot items whispered in the darkness, sighs and hisses criticizing the frivolity of the day. It snoops outside the bedroom window, tugging at your consciousness to glean more juicy items for its sardonic whispers.

The wind flaunts the rule that says it must subside with the setting sun, and once it is past that barrier, it claims the night with voodoo authority. It conspires with the moon to sow a benign madness across the undulating shadows, and in the darkness, the edges of the earth are drawn in to mark the black precipices.

Then if you would venture forth, you must free your imagination to ride with the old hags of the night wind, seeing the slinking deer as the brown cloaks of mysterious agents, and the sudden flutter of whippoorwills as desperate messages flung into the darkness by the eternally lost.

Such are the requirements of the night traveler now in the steaminess of summer. But if an emancipated imagination is proper gear, it is conditioned by a reality that is equally untethered.

So once near the middle of a hot and windy night when a trout fisherman waded slowly upstream—the cool water around his legs with serpentine caresses—there was potential for both the imagination and reality. Under the hissing cover of the night wind, progress through the water was made with the silence of a cat, and the effect was rare acceptance into the heart of the wildness.

Deeper into the countryside, as the stream wound through thick woods and weeds and bruised clouds blotted up the moon, a personal sense of location lost all precision: The twisting stream was the only tie to the "this is where I am at this point in time" condition that inhibits the rational mind.

Around a bend, where a huge willow undulated in the wind like a giant squid in a running sea, the thick vegetation broke, and the black silhouette of an ancient barn loomed just up from the stream. In the sporadic moonlight, its angular hulk dominated the oxbow bend, and then between it and the creek, the strange shadows began to emerge.

At first, only the blurred shapes of cows were apparent as the ponderous black and white beasts seemed to lunge about in confusion, their muteness broken only by an occasional grunt. Then there was something else, something smaller and more agile—a dog, a silent farm dog that darted at the cows like a tormenting wolf, its shadow moving low to the ground, then leaping suddenly to snap its jaws with the instinct of the ages.

In its closeness, the scene threatened to open like a maw, to devour everything. Then there was another shadow, of human form, arising from among the shifting beasts and waving an arm overhead. The laughter came then, something issuing from obvious dementia with a soft cackle. It was a primitive, discordant sound that sawed against your scalp like a sharp-toothed comb to make your hair stand on end. And it was the apparent encouragement that the dog needed to throw off the burden of domesticity and act out its ancestral assault.

In the midnight flicker of moonlight, it was terribly real, the shifting shadows of the beleaguered cows, the dog with its snapping jaws, and the androgynous human figure that choreographed the madness and danced about with cackling glee.

The maw opened wider, and the edge of many things was as close as it ever gets, one step away, perhaps, one more step into the hot night wind.

ONE WITH THE SHADOWS

The summer days tumble past now like acrobatic clowns, outrageous in their color, demanding childish laughter and creating the pleasant illusion of timelessness.

Within these circus days, a grand parade of bruised thunderheads marches across the land, flaunting the instruments of wind and rain, flashing batons of lightning and beating thunderous drums.

And over it all, the sun dominates, its hellish fires flicking down through the emptiness of space to be transformed by the atmosphere into that great warm breast that suckles all things.

So there is an incredible lushness, a breathless greening that is almost suffocating, and within it the shadows of the wild land become deep and dark, and they beckon like the denizens of another dimension. There is a Pied Piper invitation to rise up from seasonal lethargy and go toward those shadows, toward the unknown: Other summers? Other lives? Something instinctive and fathomless stirs deep within, as mysterious as migratory signals, as untouchable as the levitated soul.

Come to us alone, the summer shadows urge. Forsake the gregariousness of the season for this one mission of self, of indulgent introspection and transcendental meandering.

And then when you approach them, the shadows stay just out of reach, mercurial and taunting, and from the treetops, invisible crows offer cynical cheers, while blue jays whine like babies.

Insects fly against the form of your being, the annoyance proving your existence and their persistence suggesting that if you fall down here and now, finally and forever, there will be a feast for thousands on into the winter.

Where the shadows seem to be thickest—where foxes go to secret dens and wounded deer go to die so that their white bones are like spilled puzzles on the moss and leaves—here the distant yapping of a dog rides the summer breeze. Amid the soft sighs, the sound is parasitic and forlorn, an ignorant and foolish claim on time and territory. But the dog is as certain of its identity as a tent preacher, and it yaps on and on.

Then if you sit in the deepest summer shadows of the woods, as alone as an owl, the shadows seem to dissipate until you can sense your own dissolution, your separation from worldly structures so that you are as nebulous and as nothing as the shadows. And in that there is a rare and frightening peace.

If, or when, it happens that you really become one with the summer shadows, you will not know it: Only a few personal record keepers and dinner partners will acknowledge your convoluted conversion and perhaps regret it briefly.

The heat of the day comes up, as if from the molten center of the earth. You can feel it on the bottoms of your feet, and on your face like the warm breath of old summers, whispering gossip and making gentle threats.

The breeze freshens, and the shadows are sliced by wavering shafts of yellow sunlight, cut like dark cake to be served at a party of one. Then the reverie is as broken as the shadows, and the summer day is just another of those cartwheeling, cacophonous clowns.

DINNER HOURS

The late summer nights throb now with cricket song, and in the morning the dust from the insects' partying hangs in the treetops as gray mist.

To the accompanying music of the crickets, a thousand things happen in the thick blackness of the damp nights. Life and death struggles are as common as gossip. Every shadow hides something that waits to devour something else. And there is a wild pulse to it all, a mysterious beating that goes to the cellular core of things.

Raccoon families fumble their way in and out of trouble like Halloween marauders, their masks in place and their serious little eyes like obsidian marbles in an endless game. From garbage cans to grape arbors they go, snitching corn and snatching apples, then scurrying on before they are caught.

Bats do zig-zag routes to shop for the choicest insects, and their passage through the night is as unmarked as the trail of random thought.

The fox patrols among the deep shadows along the line fence, its sharp nose pointing like a casual executioner's finger: young rabbits, careless mice, a low-roosting bird. A squeak. A chirp. And a late dinner is served in the tall weeds, a la carte, with wild plums for dessert.

The owl dines, too, traveling through the damp night air on wings as silent as prayer, and sinking talons into tender morsels that protest their fate with incredibly brief contortions.

The owl and the fox go forth into the night with the grand assumption that they are to be served from the cornucopia before them. The assumption is as valid as ordering a hamburger, and no offense can be taken if some of the little death squeaks poke through bedroom windows in the night.

Sometimes the night is reluctant to let go. Then it pulls the sky down to fend off the day with a blanket of fog, and the morning is as limp and damp as a mourner's handkerchief. Then the circadian cycle wobbles a bit, and in the unsteadiness of it, the night makes a false claim. And in the deepest shadows of these sodden and somber mornings—those that could not survive the glare of the sun—sometimes the eyes of night stare out with a mournful glare. They are the eyes of the victims and the survivors, all of them parties to the great seasonal sorting.

They are there and then they are gone, and if the fog lifts it is impossible to think that they were ever there at all.

THERE WILL BE TURTLES

The snapping turtle's snout poked out of the tall grass beside the busy highway. The huge reptile, as big as a spare tire, held its sharply pointed nose high, as if it was sniffing at the stream of traffic that hissed by a few feet away.

The highway bisected the turtle's cattail-rimmed pond, slicing through it as rudely as a sidewalk in a bedroom. As is the case with birds and mammals, reptiles do not sit on committees that plan highways, and now the snapping turtle contemplated the consequences.

Within its bomb-shaped head, the turtle's small brain had no equipment for dealing with the swishing barrier before it. It programmed only the sensory messages of motion, and the line of vehicles might as well have been a stream of mastodons or a stampede of buffalo.

The turtle only knew this, and knew it with conviction enforced by the ages: It is time to propagate, to go to a place of sun-drenched sand and deposit the round, Ping-Pong ball-sized eggs; to claw out a shallow depression, lay the eggs, and then cover them in that strange way turtles have of reproducing.

But there was the highway and the hissing cars. For a long time, the snapping turtle did not move.

Years ago, a young man killed a snapping turtle in the back alley of a small town. He chopped the turtle's head off in a senseless act of mayhem, and small boys watched with awful fascination for hours as the turtle's nervous system kept it moving in slow spasms.

That dead turtle lives to this day in the memory of one of those boys, its claws pawing at the air and its blood staining the dust of the alley. It was one of those early experiences that leaves a mark, in this case a sympathy and respect for the plodding dumbness of the ugly snapping turtle.

So there was a sense of relief when the turtle beside the highway turned slowly and headed back down the slanting shoulder of the road, making its way ponderously through the tall grass like a great flea crawling about on a green dog.

The turtle would find another place to lay its eggs. The biological signals will not be denied; there will be other snapping turtles to help future generations with the meaning of ugly and primitive.

There will be other turtles, and their chances of enduring through the coming ages seem assured—much more so, in fact, than the chances for the species that juggles the explosive tools of its own self-destruction.

Perhaps one day the snapping turtle will watch as mankind performs death spasms in the dust. Then the turtle will be able to cross the highway wherever it chooses.

THE TENNIS CRICKET

What does a cricket know about tennis?

Nothing, of course.

Certainly the cricket on the court the other evening could not have known that the flop and squeak of shoes against the asphalt posed a terrible threat to its life.

Attempts to herd the cricket off to the side were futile, so it stayed in the middle of the game—assuming that our hit-swish-chase style of play can be called a game.

Maybe it was the heat of the evening—it had been an oppressively hot day—or maybe I had strained too hard returning a lob with a lob. In any case, I began to hear what sounded like a tiny voice in paroxysms of tinkling laughter.

At first I thought the faint laughter was echoing out of a nearby apartment building, but then it became obvious: It was the cricket.

There was more tinkling laughter as I sent a smashing serve into the net . . . of the adjoining court.

Another peal of bell-like laughter came faintly up from the surface of the court as I took an opponent's line drive in the stomach.

Again the laughter came as I tried to leap high enough to stop a ball that seemed to be going over my head. Actually, I misjudged the ball and it caromed off my racket handle and landed in the shrubbery outside the court.

But strangely and suddenly, there was no laughter at my latest tennis bumble.

I looked down and . . .

Yes, coming down from my ridiculous leap I had squashed the cricket flatter than a tiddlywink.

The score was love-40, and I was about to be beaten again. But I glanced down at the dead cricket, then served an ace that John McEnroe couldn't have returned.

There are morals here.

For the cricket: If you are going to laugh at someone's game, do it from the safety of the bleachers.

For those of us who blunder and fumble: If you hang in there long enough, someday the taunting laughter will stop, and all will go well.

FORTY-TWO REGULAR

In the lushness of this season, little lives and little deaths conspire. Flightless birds tumble from nests to disappear into the deep shadows. And an innocent catnap charts the close proximity of the deepest edge.

The fate of the fledglings can only be conjecture: a predators' lunch, hypothermia on a cold night, rescue by parents bearing worms and bugs.

But the nap: That can be examined, up to a point, and then it, too, becomes conjecture.

The small lake was on the bedrock wilderness like something spilled. It nestled among the sharp spires of the boreal forest, and a wind with the chill of a glacier's breath blew wrinkles onto its dark surface.

The old fishermen had gone to a bigger lake, to thread needle-sharp hooks through the heads of quivering minnows, and then to crank pike out of the depths and into a foreign medium, where the fishes' red gills convulsed with the futility of unprimed pumps. The old fishermen knew their game, and they practiced it as they had for decades, patiently and with the feel for it in their grizzled hearts and their arthritic fingers.

The younger fishermen had gone to yet another lake where the challenge was more mechanical: long outboard motor runs and beaver dam portages. They were into the chase, and its challenge was more important than the heft of a fish stringer.

And so the trek to the little sand-rimmed lake was a solitary one, made over a trail of drying mud where the tracks of moose and a large wolf were preserved like the commemorative prints of show business stars.

A large shorebird—maybe a willet—alerted the

remote lake to the intruder. It flew up from the sand and called loud and long in a voice that carried out across the water like a shout of indignation. Across the lake, ravens squawked the northern gossip that may or may not have dealt with making life from the expiration of others.

In the shallow water, minnows darted off and the vacant shell of a crayfish reposed in the leafy debris. Among the rocks, long black leeches waited, and if you soaked your bare feet or dared to take a swim, they came undulating toward the heat of your body and the bloody cocktail it promised.

The wolf had walked the shore, its prints plain in the sand. Over and beyond the tracks there was the feel of the animal, the psychic trail it had left as its predatory brain spilled out the peculiar thought process of the hunter. It marked out territory in the imagination as certainly as warm urine on a stump; and in its powerful reminder of the intruder's limitations, it produced the humility and unease of a rogue in church.

In the lee of the wind, where the blueberry bushes and the sphagnum moss grew a mattress and a big slanting jack pine made a backrest, the temptation to pause was irresistible. There was the quiet whisper of the wind, then. Just that: the soft sighs of air moving to the rotation of the earth, brushing the treetops and dipping down to sow diamonds across the lake.

A pair of loons swam nearby and were strangely silent, as was a solitary gull that drifted overhead like the ghostly flotsam of a wilderness wake.

Consciousness faltered, then walked the line, then lost the battle. And in the brief sleep, dreams and reality could not be separated. The olive and brown fishing garb blended with the shore, until the intruder was invisible even to himself, reclined in the soft moss and the coarse vegetation, and only temporarily distinguishable from the rotting log nearby.

It was like a fitting for a grave: 42-Regular. I'll take it. It is, of course, the only one that makes sense, particularly here, where the eons have not had time to put topsoil over the bedrock, and where the ravens have to eat.

Then a drake merganser came swimming past only inches away, and in its businesslike muttering there was the message to get up and get on with it, because in the hard, wild land, the imagination is just so much extraneous clutter.

THE QUIET GUEST

The considerate guest treads the summer softly, going to the wild places like a shadow, listening, watching, and leaving no tracks on the pliant green earth. It is an instinct that has been constricted by the cacophony of civilization until it is barely recognizable, but there was a time when to go quietly was to survive. Now, quietness is an "endangered species" of the human psyche, a spotted owl of an attribute that is hooted at by the noisy mob.

But there is still a payoff: The quiet guest of this season gets the catbird seat. And from this perch, the soft twittering of the goldfinch is a symphony, its four-note cadence everywhere across the overgrown pastures as the tiny birds ride the crests of invisible waves from one thistle patch to the next, and their songs float up to the silent clouds like delicate, drifting seeds.

Along the edges of hazelnut brush and blackberry briars, the song sparrow lives up to its name and dares to break the quiet of summer in such a way that it is never really broken at all.

On the pasture edge, where a great, gray stump stands as a marker for an early era of exploitation, a soft breeze leads the daisies and the black-eyed susans in a gentle dance with the tall grasses and weeds. Nearby, along the shore of a bog lake, a family of otters cavorts to the soft clucking of one of the adults. The aquatic animals are as one with the water, as if there had been a clotting of the hydrogen and oxygen molecules into sinewy blobs of energetic sleekness; and to watch them is to know some little hint of the earth's synergy.

Across the small bay in the shadows of the alder, a deer tosses its head against the tormenting flies and looks out across the lake, where a loon alternately dives and preens. The deer is growing antlers, and they protrude from its head in velvet sheaths. Within the softness, coursing blood concentrates calcium, and the antlers form into weapons for autumn's biologic battles, and into twisted little trophies to salve hunters' egos. There is no hunting season on loons, and it is an easy anthropomorphic leap to relate this fact to the crazy laughter that the bird sends reverberating across the water.

Later, an eagle comes to watch it all, perching like royalty in the dead poplar tree and flying off, finally, on great wings that seem to pump iron instead of air.

The quiet summer guest must host in kind, providing a relaxed welcome at the sudden appearance of a mink along the lake shore near the cabin. The nervous little animal tries to claim a freshly caught pike that lies on the grass beside a grinning boy who wallows in compliments. And then there is an absurd tug-of-war that the boy wins, and so the mink darts off to snitch minnows out of an open bucket until the young fisherman puts that out of reach, too.

A family of skunks were summer guests once. No, that's not accurate: The skunks lived under the cabin and were the hosts; the cabin's occupants were the guests. But it worked out: cohabitation through quiet . . . and respect, a lot of respect, except for a small dog that simply refused to accept the situation and kept everyone on edge by violating the conditions of the truce.

Once a black bear came in the summer night, sticking its snout into the garbage can and leaving such big tracks in the soft mud that in the light of the following morning, the size of the animal grew to be gargantuan; and there was a crazy impulse to telephone Bill Faulkner and say, "Get on over here and make some notes: Old Ben ain't dead after all!"

In the quiet of the night, the coarse croaking of a big

bullfrog rolls across the lake to produce a belching chorus that interfered with sleep, but now there seems to be only a few of them left.

Nothing stays the same. One summer it is skunks, another summer it is a bear. And now it is the otter and the bold, fish-hungry mink.

But something constant is emerging here, and some little correction is needed in the egocentric course: Forget the role of host, because it is absurd; when you go to meet the wild summer creatures you are always the guest. And if you do not have the good sense to be gracious and quiet, then you risk rejection and the relentless purgatory of a boom-box society.

A Calf Is Born

It was not the kind of thing you expected to get involved in on a day when summer was beginning to fray at the edges and the air had a used quality to it, as if it were weary from presiding over the seasonal rush of life cycles.

For reasons no longer remembered, I sought out Mr. Jennings on a farm nestled in the green hills, where a brook trout stream meandered like a river of diamond-studded gin. I found him—a slim, elderly man—in the barn, deeply involved in trying to help a young cow with the birth of her first calf. It was not going well: The calf was stuck in the birth canal, and while the cow strained and Mr. Jennings pulled on the protruding front feet, there seemed to be no progress whatsoever.

Obviously, you can't walk away from that kind of thing with a casual, "Well, I see you're busy, I'll come back later." So then there were three of us trying to bring the stubborn calf into the light of day: the cow, Mr. Jennings, and me.

The cow had no clear understanding of our role in the matter, and from where she lay in the yellow straw, she would look back over her shoulder periodically with a sad, accusatory look in her big, bovine eye. We would pull on the rope fastened to the calf's front feet, the cow would strain, and except for the sweat that streamed down our faces, nothing much happened.

Mr. Jennings was worried. This kind of thing could go on only so long, and then there was danger to the calf and the cow. He had been through this before. Most farmers have, but it is a nerve-wracking and exhausting experience. He said he had better call the veterinarian, but we went back at it, pulling so hard on the calf that it seemed we would tear it apart.

It went on and on, and just when it seemed that we were totally defeated, a fraction of an inch of progress could be seen. It was a catalyst for greater effort, at least for Mr. Jennings and me, and we pulled as if our lives depended on it as much as the cow's and the calf's.

In retrospect, there cannot be many times that were as totally absorbing as those moments. It somehow seemed that nothing else really mattered, and that it was incredibly important that the calf be born.

And then it happened. Suddenly, the calf slipped into the straw-strewn world as if it had just been invited. It came so easily and so suddenly that it sent Mr. Jennings and me sprawling.

We got to our feet and Mr. Jennings inspected the calf and pronounced it alive and well. Then we stood there and admired "our" handiwork.

It seems safe to speak for Mr. Jennings as well as myself and say that our spirits were buoyed way out of proportion to the occurrence. It is possible, of course, that even peripheral participation in a birth is tremendously meaningful to males, given their denial of anything of real significance in that area.

It may seem excessive to recall with such fondness the birth of a dumb animal that has long since gone to hamburger, but I remember that when I left the Jennings farm that day, the late summer did not seem so frayed, nor the air so weary.

THE SILENT BIRDS

Now we are in that time when the summer takes on a breathless silence. It is as if the lushness of the vegetation has worked, sponge-like, on the birds and the creatures and soaked them up like so many crumbs.

To stand quietly in the woods or the fields now is like being center stage in an empty theater. The orchestra, the audience, the performers, all of them seem to be gone, and there is the vague feeling that it was a tremendous show, but it is over, and only the lavish scenery remains. The only sound is the droning of the crickets, tiny marchers in a monotonous band too miniscule to see.

Since most of the wild creatures are mute except in intimate whimpering and grunting among themselves, the absence of the birds is most noticeable. During the spring and early summer, when the birds were dividing up territories and raising families, there was a constant cacophony of chirps and whistles and squawks. It began in the pre-dawn darkness and continued through the day, ending with the lusty claim of a robin or cardinal getting in the last birdy word at dusk from a topmost branch.

But now there is nothing. Even the raucous crows have clammed up like the indicted. They make their feeding patrols as silently as witches, and then they disappear.

Where are all the birds? Is it safe to assume that they are loafing and preening behind the curtain of thick grass and leaves, building stores of bodily energy for long migratory flights or to survive the long winter?

Perhaps. But it is also possible to imagine them all gathered in secret places, in great chattering assemblies where they discuss in indignant tones the hazards of pesticides and flight path obstructions and the expansion of asphalt and concrete over the surface of the earth.

It is also possible to expand that fantasy and concentrate the energy of a billion tiny brains and muscular breasts in an assault on the arrogance of the species that does these awful environmental things in the name of progress. Hitchcock only scratched the feathery surface.

There is a mystery in these quiet days of late summer. In the absence of the birds, a monumental question is posed: What in the world is going on? We seem to have a breakdown of the natural cycle, a pause that cannot be programmed in a system that demands an action and a reaction for every second of every minute of every day.

The answer is obvious, and if we miss it, it is only because some parts of us are loafing and hiding with the birds. Everything is still going on. It is just that the pace has slowed down. Frenzy has been replaced by subtlety, screeches by whispers, fights by compromise, powerful reproductive urges by routine daily hunger.

The great pecking order has been reasserted, among species and from species to species; and sometimes in the silent, questioning days of the lush season that is pregnant with collapse, the real question has to be whether or not we deserve to place ourselves on top.

It's enough to make us as quiet as the birds.

ONE FOR THE CRICKETS

Now, in the moderating days of a summer of drought, this is how the season must be remembered.

The summer mornings came on in a steely haze. The sun glared red on the horizon, like the bloody eye of madness, then rose slowly to begin its burn.

In its unfailing ascension and its relentless fire there was an invitation to misery, a summons to work a shift among the furnaces of this cheerless foundry of a summer.

Children, as limp as worms, lolled in bed to delay their daily sun dance. They emerged at mid-morning, gangly zombies hatched from rumpled sheets, and they stumbled to pools and beaches.

The adults coped. Road and construction workers toiled beneath the blazing sun like ants condemned to carry crumbs in the ovens of hell. Others rode air-conditioned vehicles to air-conditioned buildings; they were like the unborn in cool wombs, gestating comfortably through the hellish days.

Across the farmland, where tomorrow's soup kettles boiled dry in an orgy of meteorologic futures, despair ran deeper than the roots of the dying corn. When the land is shaved annually in the name of agronomic respectability, it is as vulnerable to the searing sun as a naked baby. Its cries of agony were in the whispering of the afternoon wind that rustled the dead leaves of things as it passed by.

The wild land fared better as the dry, torrid season built to a climax, but it too displayed signs of distress. Oak wilt and other diseases mounted successful assaults, and trees died with slow certainty, like soldiers fading away. Smaller plants collapsed like crumpled napkins, and the song of the cicada mocked it all with a toneless, incessant buzz.

The niggardly music of this summer filtered down out of

the haze in the soft twittering of goldfinches. It was even more tentative than usual, like delicate flower petals of sound that barely held together to reach the earth.

The tiny birds with their characteristic flap-'em-and-fold-'em flight were invisible against the glare of the sun. Maybe they were up there and maybe they weren't. Maybe their song was left over from another summer, when such cheerful sound seemed easier to come by.

Along a tiny, twisting stream, where wild sunflowers, ironweed, and meadow rue defied the drought to grow tall and thick, a grasshopper flung itself into the air from a stalk of canary grass. It was not possible to know the grasshopper's plan, but certainly it was not to land on the cool, swirling surface of the water, then to kick-swim a couple of strokes and end life suddenly in the gaping jaw of a small brook trout. In the choking dryness of the summer, the watery event involving the grasshopper and the trout was somehow reassuring: The processes and the cycles go on, and eventually the rains will come to orchestrate a great natural revival.

In the shade of a birch cluster along a tired line fence, a family of sandhill cranes rested and preened. They had fed through the alfalfa, using their long beaks to pluck insects with surgical precision, and there was nothing to do now but survive the torrid day and to be around to greet the dawn of the next one with a magnificent yodel.

The sun turned bright red again as it sank to the horizon. It poised there, a balloon of fire reluctant to leave the steamy party that it has hosted.

The hot day ended, like a tire going slowly flat. A final soft sigh moved the tops of the trees, then it was still as death. From somewhere, a cricket rushed into the audio void. Then there were others, and the night was given over to them. In their cheerful chirping, there was a sound of celebration, as if the crickets rejoiced at surviving yet another blistering summer day.

THE ESSENCE OF CHANGE

This is the most sensuous of times. Late summer is always like that, going beyond sights and sounds and smells, and begging to be touched and tasted.

Wild plums are offered like rosy, puckered lips, and to reach up into the hot afternoon sunshine to retrieve them is to claim the sweet kiss of the season.

Clusters of elderberries bow down with their own extravagance, like wine that is aged just right, and you can "drink" them until purple juice drips down your shirt front and an exquisite intoxication sets in.

Untended apple trees flaunt their commercial freedom and tease to be tasted by those who like the challenge of an occasional small worm.

Down in the shadows, where briars guard them like barbed wire, shiny, lush blackberries are epicurean jewels that invite the groping hand and then scratch it bloody.

Everywhere, the fruit and the berries ripen—along the trails and in the forgotten orchards and pastures—and except for that consumed by the birds and the wild critters and the occasional passerby who stops to gorge or gather a basketful for making jam, it all falls to the earth in soft rustling and gentle plops, or in the harsh sway of summer storms. And if we think it's a waste, then our species-centric nature has become intolerable.

In a river bottom, far away from the arteries of commerce and hidden from even the casual wanderer, a half dozen cardinal flowers poke up out of the greenery as brilliant shafts of the brightest red. Out of the black muck of the river's ever-shifting silt, the plant has used the summer sun to produce spectacular, blossom-laden stems. They are like warning flares: Danger! I am this flower in this time. I do not care if you see me or not. But if you do, remember me and the bounty of this summer. Because if you forget it all, what was the point of your having been here, or anywhere?

Millions of bees and other insects work the bergamot and touch-me-not and cone flowers and the late-blossoming weeds. In their apparent aimless wandering, there is such purpose and dedication as to make a sham of our grand plans. Each insect is programmed to a precise goal on a very specific spot on the earth, and it works steadily until it drops dead. It is the nature of all things. The insect is protected from the harsh truth of this by ignorance. Our only protection is a sense of humor.

The sun presides now over layers of gray haze that are on the land as the mysterious steam and vapor of the great natural factory. In the morning, the sun rises like a red ball bouncing slowly up from a Hades game; and in the evening, it sets with a reluctant sizzle, sometimes flaring wide across a cloud formation as if it is feigning an escape from the universe.

In the wake of the sun, there is the momentous circadian adjustment. Night approaches, and all living things must make an accommodation. Chemical processes slow, defenses go up, shelter is sought. A tiny yellow-throat does some last-minute feeding deep down in the canary grass and iron weed, emerging occasionally with its black-masked face to check the waning of the day. A nuthatch calls; a pileated woodpecker makes a last· cackling flight over the creek bottom and disappears into the shadows of the white pine.

Thousands of tiny flies hatch to hover over the creek, some so small as to be invisible and each one with its own complex agenda. A trout begins to feed daintily, its light little splashes like the dancing of a fairy.

A red squirrel chatters. A catbird calls from back in

the alder. And a wren flutters to a mud flat for a cold-water nightcap. Then a stillness settles over it all, the kind of pause that is never possible until the season advances so that crickets mark the evening temperature.

And in that pause, there is something even beyond the sensuous—something terribly personal and totally metamorphic. As a mayfly emerges from its earliest casing, we shed the shell of another year; and out of the seasonal lushness and its relentless time keeping, the essence of autumn's melancholia drifts as light as thistle seeds.

THE SUMMER'S LITTER

The summer ended too soon, slipping off in the gray rain with no more fanfare than an anonymous drifter. It disappeared behind its own green curtain, and in the slow shuffle of its departure, all things marked personal time, in particular the newly hatched snapping turtles and the faltering man along the country trail.

As usual, there were a thousand loose ends, things undone, things delayed. Beside the trail, wildflowers blossomed beyond their season; late-hatching birds built flight muscle; and long after all the others were bare of fruit, one elderberry bush produced thick, lush berries that came to the palate like tiny casks of wine: Summer's Essence, 1991.

Flocks of olive-colored goldfinches, having spent the richness of their plumage on seasonal extravagance, came up out of the brown weeds to fill the cooling air with their twittering, bobbing flight. A swarm of blackbirds, in a synchronized formation of infinite grace, alighted in the top of a tall cottonwood. The birds were there like a sudden crop of alien fruit and then, individually and in twos and threes, they began to drop down to the cattails, having somehow switched from their collective chorus-line number to individual performances by way of a signal known only to them.

Roosters crowed. From a fence-line thicket, a rooster pheasant announced its presence with the voice that always sounds as if it is being forced backwards across strained vocal cords. And from a farm yard, domesticated roosters made their raucous little speeches with the arrogance of unopposed politicians.

A goshawk launched itself from its dead-tree perch

and sailed off in the direction of the crowing. The hawk is, of course, indifferent to the concept of property rights as it pertains to roosters. It does, in fact, demonstrate that it is all absurd except that a rooster can be "owned" only by that entity which renders it into dinner.

In the hard flatness of the trail's surface, there were cold dinners for a multitude of diners. Dead grasshoppers lay here and there along the weedy edges, the careless soldiers of August that could not pattern their grand leaps to escape the seasonal advance. Lifeless earthworms, their rain-induced missions turning them into casualties, were strewn everywhere, and not only the "early bird" could gorge.

And then, in the middle of the trail, as vulnerable to hungry birds and critters as the grasshoppers and the worms, was a tiny snapping turtle. Hardly bigger than a quarter but looking exactly like the formidable adults of its species, the turtle had apparently just hatched. The miniature reptile, its head extended, struggled slowly over the gravel surface.

Then two more of them were spotted nearby, the same size and equally as vulnerable to the hundreds of predatory life forms in the river bottom.

It was too much temptation for the species that cannot mind its own business in natural matters and therefore manipulates and tinkers uncontrollably: The tiny turtles were picked up and placed on the muddy riverbank under the shelter of the bridge.

Was that a better place for them than the open trail? Were they hatched so late for a reason? Were they meant to survive into a life that is protected from almost everything by the armor-like shell of their kind, or were they only to serve as dinner for something else?

The summer had left a litter of questions. But as they were pondered, there was the disheveled man, emerging unexpectedly from the woods to walk unsteadily along the trail. His face was blotched and dripping with perspiration; and behind their puffiness, his eyes were red and watery. He went hesitantly, stopping often to look down into the weeds as if he had lost something. A bottle, perhaps? Or was he there in sickness of another kind?

The ailing man's presence seemed disharmonious to the litany of natural circumstances that marked the subtle departure of summer. He could be ignored for purposes of picturesque prose, but that would somehow be an even worse kind of manipulation than moving the turtles.

He was there. The birds were there. The turtles were there. We were there. In all of it, there was a completeness to the transitional statement. It went to the dichotomous certainty and uncertainty of seasonal endings, and nature would not suffer kindly the censoring of it all.

Autumn

Melancholy Owl

The seasonal signals are out there now, in a dimension we cannot really know. We feel the summer temperatures break. We see the incredible chlorophyll metamorphose begin. We hear the chirps and clucks and cries of migrating birds. We can even taste the transition in the crisp crunch of apples and the sweetness of shiny grapes.

All of these sensory messages come to us with the subtlety of carnival barkers, and we are before them like children, clutching our psyche coins in sweaty fists and wondering how to get on the merry-go-round.

In our rush to come down out of the trees and emerge from the caves, we left behind whatever it is that tunes a life form in to the seasonal cycle. Instead of a clear signal, now we get static, and within it melancholia breeds like the green lichens of autumn.

In the morning, mist rises slowly up off the rivers in swirls of gray reluctance, swaddling the senses and the spirit; and to be enveloped there is to regress into a wispy amniotic state, where everything floats in grand ethereal turbulence.

Great flocks of blackbirds rise out of this low cloudiness to wheel across the brown seas of beans and corn on the passive prairie. The sound of their beating wings is like the teasing of a strange seiche, and in their gregarious flocking they broadcast the message of seasonal inclusion and belonging. There is a taunting in it for the outsider.

In the heat of the day, heat as tentative now as a rejected suitor, butterflies do their last tangos; and when the thermals build in the afternoon, flocks of sandhill cranes ride them like elevators until the big birds are only dots against the blue, and their wild yodels are drowned in the high river of winds. Then they sail off into an exclusive oblivion, and the observer is left to contemplate the emptiness of the spacious sky.

The sun burns down to the horizon in a red glow, rests there for a second, then is gone, sinking as unceremoniously as a good idea gone bad. In the gathering dusk, crickets discuss the temperature with the precision of scientists, and nighthawks begin their patrols, riding their blade-like wings in a zig-zag harvest of flying bugs.

Then in the night, with the stars winking over the old joke of earthly egotism, millions of tiny birds emerge from trees and shrubs to resume their nocturnal trips to winter places. They fly as unerringly as navigators, their traffic patterns perfect and their flight plans flawless. Sometimes, in very quiet places, you can hear some of them, an occasional chirp drifting down from a darkened sky. But mostly it is only a matter of knowing they are up there, flying off mysteriously through the night, alone and together.

Later, the yelp of snow geese filters down, far away and so faint that it might be mistaken for the cries of complaining puppies. It is gone then, and still later, when the night is on the land like a habit, a screech owl sends its quavering call out of the deep shadows. It is borrowed as a seasonal summation for an inarticulate expatriate. In its mournful ebb and flow, it expresses the haunting regret for having lost some part of autumn too nebulous for definition.

EARTHBOUND

The ghosts of summer are running up and down the brown corn rows now, rattling the drying leaves and hissing at each other in a game of seasonal tag. The corn stalks are as tall and strong as trees, brought to that condition by a warm, wet summer that would encourage a fence post to sprout limbs and leaves.

The squirrels are finally done with the hickory tree in the front yard, having stripped it of every last nut as they kept the driveway littered with hulls for the past month or more. The squirrels don't seem to be burying the nuts, as tradition dictates, but rather eating them on the spot. Is it possible that the squirrels' lifestyle has changed to reflect that of their human neighbors?

One last cricket can be heard through the bedroom window, its song slow-paced and laced with sadness. Perhaps it laments the fact that it missed the big cricket orgy of the past month and now knows the despair of rejection and regret.

The jack-in-the-pulpit is offering its cluster of scarlet berries as a marker of the season, and the snake weed is making a white-blossomed statement about its worth among the backyard day lilies.

A great tidal wave of brown, more powerful than anything the moon could produce, moves across the countryside now. It fills the low places first, inundates the valleys, and climbs to the tops of the highest hills. Brown is not as clannish as green, which claims the summer for its many-hued family. The brown of autumn invites along its rowdy friends of yellow, orange, red, amber, and many other colors, and they have a party to which everything and everyone is invited.

In the certainty of seasonal signals, given in concert to most species, man and his family stand as uncomprehending and unresponsive as clip-winged dolts. Confused and distressed by the bustle all about, they are only awkward observers.

Cries and yelps come down from laden skies, and the soft whisper of wingbeats is everywhere. One autumn day, the sandhill cranes gathered in a pasture, an awesome reunion of huge, cackling birds. They stood tall, stuttering and strutting, and there was all about an air of celebration, of acknowledging the crop of young, of renewing acquaintances, of discussing plans for exciting travel on the thermals of tomorrow.

Later in the woods, halfway up an oak tree where the view of the cranes was the best, one of those awkward observers sat like a giant tree frog and watched it all. Then suddenly the cooling afternoon sunshine was thick with fluttering, clucking blackbirds, thousands and thousands of them, descending into the trees like strange peppery seasoning. There could be no organization to it, and yet it was choreographed perfectly, each bird in its place and chirping its appropriate song. They perched on every limb of every tree, as unaware of the hulking observer who sat among them as bees of a stone. In their fluttering, flowing movement, they passed within inches, and the noise of their wings was like thunder muted beneath millions of tiny black feathers.

In the midst of the blackbirds, the messages of the seasons came to the observer with an astounding and inspirational clarity, but there was confusion, too. The truth was, he could not read the signals: They were not in his frequency. They would have him soar like the cranes or fly like the blackbirds, when by evolutionary circumstance, he was capable only of falling to the earth like the hull of a hickory nut.

Therein may lie the source of autumn's melancholia.

THE HARVEST

The great harvest has been going on for weeks now. Lesser creatures—squirrels and muskrats, for example—know of it and act accordingly, building stores of fat and food and preparing shelters. Without this "harvesting," they would not survive.

As a species, we tend to ignore the harvest. From where we cling precariously to the highest rung, such mundane activity no longer seems worthy of our attention.

But now, across the prairies and the rolling hills of the country, machines as big as small houses lumber up and down the rows of corn and beans. Sometimes, on a bright autumn day, you can see the glistening of last summer's sun on the kernels of grain that spill out of the machines and into the wagons and trucks.

The machines envelop themselves in clouds of dust and plant debris. In their ponderous movement and complicated function, they seem somehow to have achieved a life of their own, independent even of the people who operate them.

Such autonomous machines begin the denial of our relationship with the harvest. Once there were those among us who knew of hands-on harvesting: cold, chapped hands ripping ears of corn from the stalks and pitching them one by one into board-sided wagons, while a biting wind hissed out of the northwest.

These same people knew the backbreaking heft of a sack of fresh grain as it was carried up the granary steps and hoisted into a storage bin.

And the intimacy of such harvest experience was somehow communicated to the rest of society, so that even the city people had some understanding of the harvest's demands and importance.

But now, except for that brief glimpse we may get of the grain pouring between the combine and the truck as we drive by, we are so removed mechanically and geographically from the harvest that we virtually deny its existence. Ours is a supermarket mentality, and the harvest for us is a grocery cart that we follow up and down the aisles.

From that perspective, it becomes increasingly difficult to remember that we are still tied to the earth with an umbilical cord as simple and as critical, in the final analysis, as the squirrel's or the muskrat's.

We would die without the harvest, like butterflies that fly too high and are swept out to sea.

Awaiting the Claw

Even now, when the sunshine can be as warm on your back as a caress, the recipe for winter is being reviewed in the north country.

Up beyond the Great Lakes, where the bedrock wears a crew cut of spruce, and the moss underfoot is thicker than the carpet of kings, there is a certain stirring, a subtle shift of focus away from the moment to the future, and to the preparations that must be made for it.

A family of loons claims the sparkling water of a quiet bay, and in the wild, quavering calls of the adults you can imagine a plea to the half-grown young: Hurry, eat fish so you will be big enough for the migratory flight before the ice comes.

But in the universal indifference of youth to the tilt of the earth, the young loons loaf and occasionally climb aboard a parent's back for a relaxed ride.

A solitary eagle, its white head like an avian crown, perches high over its empty nest, and with psychic powers tuned high to perceive the moodiness of autumn, you can hear the great bird asking: Where has the summer gone? Where are the offspring I raised? Will they know enough to find open water so they can survive the winter?

In a little town with an Indian name, the baying of bear hounds comes galloping across the lake in a vocal stampede. The dogs' presence means, of course, that some of the north country bears will not know the seasonal nap of hibernation but rather that deepest of sleeps that awaits all things.

The seasonal ritual that is involved, when predatory lust swims like leeches in the veins of men, extends to the moose, and now those lumbering, sponge-muzzled monsters must keep to the thickets or spend the winter as hard little packages in a hunter's freezer.

Here and there along the shores of the wilderness lakes, a maple shrub has burst into seasonal flame, and birch trees are paying off the growing season mortgage with coins of leafy gold.

Soon there will be enough color for a party, and one day the parade of clouds over the spruce spires will spit a confetti of snow, instead of cold rain. Then the pileated woodpecker will cackle a farewell to its migratory brethren as the loons take off like bush planes, circle once, and head south.

But however bright the color, it is only as insignificant splashes on the great green blotter of the north. Dark green and shadows dominate, always the dark shadows, never quite erased by the bright summer sun and waiting like a secret army to occupy the land with bully muscles during the months of long nights.

Now the signals are here in the far north. The tilt is on, the sun sinks lower, and the shadows of the north country are sneaking and creeping down over the Canadian border. One day the caress of the sun on your back will have a claw in it. Then you will know that the shadows are coming, and it is time to choose; retreat like the loon or hold to the cold ground like the pileated woodpecker.

FILLET OF SOUL

The late afternoon was slipping away like a thief, taking the golden sunshine from the aspen trees and changing the blood red of the sumac to clotted shadows. It was a crime of time that seemed particularly bad, because it had been such a fine autumn day and now on the country hill where the Vermont Lutheran Church stood in solitary, sunwashed splendor, there was a subliminal urge to hang on to the day—to grasp the fading light and wring more warmth out of it.

But the sun alone had not warmed this day in this vicinity. It had something else going for it on the Wisconsin hilltop where the road curved in front of the church before dropping off into the wooded hills. This was the day of the annual lutefisk and meatball supper, and all day long people had bustled about in preparations and participation.

Beginning in the early afternoon, people began to drive out from the nearby towns and villages, winding along the quiet roads and marveling at the brilliant colors of the trees.

At the church there was always a wait, but nobody minded. The pause provided a chance to stroll through the beautiful graveyard behind the church, to walk among the Johnsons and Olsons and the other Scandinavians resting beneath the trees and the sod. Sometimes children ran and romped among the headstones, but they meant no disrespect, and if there had been a way to communicate it, the permanent residents probably would have given such activity their enthusiastic approval.

You could get a cup of coffee at a small tent next to the church—free, of course—and the man who offered it would tell you about the lutefisk and smile at the lutefisk jokes he has heard a thousand times.

In the interests of organization, the guests wait briefly in the church itself, sitting in the polished pews and looking at the magnificent white altar. Sometimes one of the ladies will play the piano, perhaps a medley of show tunes, something like "Anything Goes," and the waiting people will smile and applaud.

Then, in turn, the guests go down into the warm, bright basement to sit at the long tables, where smiling women in white dresses and little red hats serve heaping platters of fish and meatballs and potatoes and green beans.

It is a wonderful meal, though not all the guests are enthusiastic about the lutefisk. All the eating is accompanied by friendly talk with old friends and family, and it is topped off with pie and coffee and a rich Norwegian dessert made from cream and sprinkled with cinnamon.

Then it ends, and the cool night is down over the church like a comforter. Overhead, the stars have never been brighter, and the air has never been fresher.

And if some "productions" that have been done recently in the name of religion bring a frown to the face of the Almighty (TV examples come to mind), then the kind of thing that went on here at the Vermont Lutheran Church must certainly make Him smile.

THINGS TRAPPED

The trappers were suddenly on the river that autumn, as if they had been macabre predators emerging out of the tannin-colored water. One day, the two of them sloshed upstream with burlap bags full of traps slung over their shoulders; the next day, they were back on the grassy bank, crouched next to a mound of dead muskrats.

That's where the schoolboys found them on an afternoon when gray clouds shrouded the bottomland and brightly colored leaves floated down the river as the discarded currency of a spendthrift season.

A foreboding autumnal essence was along the river that day, the old warning that the season can never be defined, and that in its profound biologic transformation of all things, the unexpected and the ominous lie in wait. The river came slithering down its wooded valley in serpentine silence, sliding past the black mud where the springs festered up, and slipping around the corpses of giant trees that settled regally and ever so slowly toward watery graves.

There was a place up the river called "the dead waters," where a tributary stream sprawled over a swamp of bottomless muck, and where neighborhood lore held that cows and horses and even a witless pioneer youth had sunk to their doom over the years. Sometimes the neighborhood boys would sit on the high hill over the dead waters and think about the bones down in the black slurry, and even on hot summer days, little spidery chills would scurry up their spines.

The boys knew a lot about the river, and they had a proprietary feeling about it. It was theirs, they felt, in its mystery and its naturalness, in its sometimes contrary ways and its seasons; and they felt a curious kinship with its creatures.

All of this was in them that day when they stood looking down at the trappers and the dead muskrats. The trappers glanced up at the boys from behind ragged whiskers, and they grinned briefly before bending over the task of skinning their grotesque catch. Their square fingers moved quickly over the shiny, matted fur, the bright little knife blades flashing like needles and the muskrats' dead eyes watching it all with sublime indifference.

The pelts were tugged off like underwear; then the muskrats were obscenely naked, and their meat-red carcasses were tossed into the river to go twisting slowly off with the current, like the fetuses of aliens.

The schoolboys watched in silence, the image imprinting like brands on their young brains until they would see it all as long as they lived—even a half-century later, when it was no longer the stuff of sinister dreams but just something stored away in a musty mental attic.

The trappers were strangers, apparently nomadic in their overnight river stops, and that set them apart in the minds of the boys from the staid and steady men of the rural community as certainly as if they had been gunfighters. Then one of the trappers looked up and made a crude inquiry about the virtue of the boys' teacher. It was so unexpected and so outlandish that it almost made the boys step back, as if the trapper had swished his knife under their noses.

The trapper laughed, a cackling laugh that went up the river hollow and hung over the cattails and the canary grass and the twisting course of the stream.

The trapper laughed again, tossing a skinned carcass into the river and poking an elbow at his partner. Then he told the boys how a teacher once kept him after school to satisfy her sexual desires, and he said it so crudely that the words were like live bugs in the country boys' ears.

It was quiet then, just the soft gurgle of the river and the cushioning gray of the afternoon coming to the senses.

The boys drifted off, finally, their pubescent minds sorting through the debris of the day. The river would never be quite the same for them; some economic factor had lashed out to insult it, and they would never forget the skinned carcasses drifting off with the current.

And even though their teacher was an old lady with her hair in a bun and with flabby upper arms, they could not look at her without thinking of the trappers.

THE LITTLE DEATHS

There is a little death for everything in the autumn cold, if you choose to see it that way—a haunting chill that clings as the frost of mortality. Dead leaves are underfoot like the cast-off currency of a world that collapsed from summer extravagance, and to walk through their crispness is to sense your own seasonal expenditure and the finite limitations on your reserves.

In the woods now, all things are ready. Unencumbered by the curse of reason with its built-in potential for procrastination, thousands of life forms have instinctively prepared for that time when the earth tilts away from the power of the sun like a child's ball spinning into shadow.

There is a sense of that now among the barren trees. A tough quiet emanates up out of the dark, humus soil where the intertwining roots delicately package the mystery of future seasons. Twisted within it down there, invisible and organized beyond our comprehension, are all of the things that we are and that everything is. Now, beneath the leaves, it all awaits the cold that will turn it as hard as stone, taking it into that part of the cycle that the ego sees as little deaths, but which is only the eternal synchronized meshing of the universe, and is therefore life itself.

Not all of it, of course, is hidden now in the moist, cooling particles of darkness and decay and fungi and worms under the leaves. There are the great, complicated creatures that have risen out of the eons to carry the banners of this ebbing time. They come on padded paws and sharp hooves to patrol the woods by night, their feet whispering a trail of secrets into the brittle leaves. They have been fitted by evolution with thick, shiny coats, and nourished by the lush season to carry layers of fat on their ribs. In their physical impressiveness and intelligence, they are the royalty of late autumn: queen wolves, prince foxes, and king deer. The woods is theirs now, really theirs, and the restraint of their instinctive behavior calls into question the excesses of the rational intellect.

Each night, the wolf hunts for rabbits in the thickets, sniffing and listening like a surgical shopper. Along the line fence, the black nose of the fox locates mice with equal facility. The pounces and the chases are part of the brisk nights. The little screams and the squeaks go out across the darkness as punctuation in the endless saga. It goes on around us every night, unfailingly, and when the cold moves over the land with a mystical stillness, sometimes tiny fragments of it come to the ear, like shrill, remote notes from instruments that play in an orchestra beyond our perception.

So the cooling earth feeds the small and the vulnerable to the predators now, and that is the balance of it; from the soil to the seeds to the seed eaters to the eaters of the seed eaters. Nothing rises above the common origin.

But sometimes now in the glory of its biologic drive, the buck deer seems almost to break the bond, standing tall and exquisitely balanced over the ground, then soaring off in magnificent leaps as if it were an entity with no natural discipline, an ethereal something with polished antlers and a lust-swollen neck. The deer dances a reckless ballet—no choreography directs and dictates the power of the reproductive urge. And if it survives the hunting season, the raging of its hormones subsides, and its antlers fall off to return the calcium to the soil from whence it came.

If it does not survive, the deer's blood drains into the soil at the hunter's feet, and the natural attachment to the earth is reaffirmed.

Now, if in the quiet autumn cooling, in the crumbling leaves, the little squeaks, the leaping deer; if in all of this, the chill of the season is seen to have only moribund trappings, it is an illusion. The ego blurs our focus, so that we have problems viewing the little endings without getting personal. The grand cycle goes on with us or without us, and this time of chilly transition is as much a cause for celebration as the blossoming of spring.

DEAF RABBITS

For all of their big ears, rabbits are very poor listeners, especially when it comes to taking advice and heeding warnings.

Since early spring, I have been telling them that one day the hawks would come, and then there would be hell to pay. Their reaction to my admonitions has been to scamper off momentarily into the weeds along the trail, then to reemerge almost as soon as I am past, thereupon to resume their business of taking the sun, lolling in the dusting hollows, and playing games of leap rabbit. They have appeared to be totally engrossed in such frivolity, and entirely unmindful of danger and threat, particularly from the peaceful sky.

In the spring dawns, when the former railroad track was just beginning to weave summer's protective maternal smock of weeds and grasses, the rabbits were so numerous that perhaps they were somehow convinced of their invincibility through sheer numbers, a dangerous, safety-in-numbers inclination common to many species, including our own.

As the summer came on and leaves replaced blossoms, the rabbits grew bigger, and if there were fewer of them, it was not readily apparent. The larger rabbits seemed emboldened by their heft and survival, and sometimes they would stand their ground until the last second before hopping off into the weeds as the bicycle hissed past.

You had better watch it, I told them. You're going to be hawk dinner as sure as your eyes are brown.

They didn't listen. And though I was not speaking their language, I imagined they heard and understood me, but chose to ignore advice from the spokesman for a species that somehow managed to out-evolve its natural enemies, but then made one of itself.

The season bogged down in biologic excess— vegetation so lush and heavy that it collapsed in on itself and there were bumper crops of everything, including rabbits. Generations followed generations, and interspersed with the grown and half-grown rabbits were more little ones, one-gulpers for the foxes and coyotes, easy swallows for the pine snakes, and simple disassembly for the owls.

But in the morning, the surviving rabbits of all sizes would be out there in the open, away from the protective dew-drenched tangle of tall, leafy plants and out there on the smooth trail surface, where even a clumsy hawk could pluck them like ripe berries.

And one morning when fat, shiny choke cherries hung over the trail and begged to be wine, the hawks were there. They had come on the wind, riding it as quietly and purposefully as the falcons of Azrael. One of them perched on the branch of a dead willow, looking as well-fed and sanctified as a rural preacher. Another soared high over the trail, making lazy circles and peering down as a gourmand might survey a smorgasbord.

I told you! I told you!

But the rabbits weren't listening.

It is just as well, of course. They have had the eons to fine-tune their genetic alarms about such things as hawks, and if they ever got it down perfectly, it would be catastrophic to the food chain and the natural harmony that includes all things. Also, the world would be overrun with rabbits.

So, when I stopped to sample the blackberries along the trail, I now talked to the hawks: Welcome to the rabbit trail, and bon appetit.

WHAT THE BUGS HEARD

Each year about this time, several box-elder bugs gather in my work space, apparently looking for compatible company, if not guidance to get through the approaching winter. On a recent afternoon, as they lounged on the sun-drenched windowsill, the following is what they heard:

My friends, we are gathered here once again in this season of transition, summer in a shambles at our feet and winter cracking its knuckles just over the hill. We are here only by dint of dumb luck, since any one of us could have been annihilated in traffic or done in by a picnic hamper. We appreciate our good fortune, and we make the audacious assumption that it will continue.

As usual, the summer went too fast, careening past in a kaleidoscope of frenzied good times and leaving us a little dazed and breathless. We gather ourselves now to rest near sunny windowsills, while the computers within us sort and "save" the bright remnants for the quilt of our memory.

We note the grand cycle now, remembering with laughter and tears the ritual and ceremonies of June brides, August births, and September funerals. We subliminally plot our own course through it all, then we are mildly puzzled by the dichotomous waves of joy and sadness that wash over us.

But enough of this kneading of the past: The summer is gone, and now we are poised here before winter as sheep to the shearing. If, my friends, I had six legs and wings as you do, I think I might seriously consider running or flying off to the south, there to bask in the warm fragrance of tropical breezes. That you winter here in the Midwest is, of course, your own biologic business. That I winter here is perhaps as naturally ordained: Somebody, I suppose, has to pay the heating bills so that we don't all freeze to death.

As usual, the world outside of us is in a quandary, brandishing obscene swords here and there, playing a ridiculous game of hot-potato with financial responsibility, wringing its hands over the chaos in inner cities, and swooning periodically over the machinations of some show biz ding-a-ling. In its proper perspective, however, all of this is little more than light entertainment, something to fret about in social settings and to occupy the media. With the exception of those directly involved, none of it is personal—not close to the heart or the head or the stomach.

What is personal, and what matters, is our perching here like penguins on the edge of an icy winter, assaying the moment as if it were something very special. And indeed it is. We are here. That is the part that is "special." Beyond that, nothing really matters, and once that overriding fact is assimilated, we can move on to the incidentals of keeping warm and well-fed and comfortable through the coming season.

So, my friends, we have this time in this place, and we have each other. And after the fact of our own existence, that is where it truly is, in our feelings for others, which in its ultimate we have labeled love. Going into the winter with some of that makes a sham of migration and hibernation.

Therefore, do I love you, you red-bellied little creepers? Ha! You're on my windowsill, aren't you? And I'm paying the heating bill.

THE PASSENGER

The sides of the valley were so steep that they seemed to close overhead to form a tunnel through the black, sodden night. It was warm and humid, and the car windows were down, so that the darkness came in with damp hissing, like sighing whispers from the gossiping dead.

The road shared the bottom of the valley with a tiny stream, joining it occasionally at small bridges where vines came twisting up to grapple with rusty steel railings, and where wet leaves lay flat on the asphalt, like the remnants of a road-killed summer.

The yellow punch of the headlights was as feeble against the ebony night as a candle, and no more effective in altering the foreboding circumstance than a whimper on the gallows.

Nobody lived in the valley. For miles, there had been no lighted windows along the winding road, and no other travelers had come along to share the twists and turns.

The hum of the car engine had faded to silence, and then there was the sensation of being in a vacuum, of floating along the edge of your own existence—as alone as you could ever get.

Then, just as the road began a laborious slither up one side of the valley, it happened: There was something in the car. A presence, yet not a presence. Something as formless as mist, yet as certain as pain. It came in from all directions, with an entrance of such exquisite grace that it escaped all notice.

It—this "something" passenger—perched on the car seat like a scowling raven. It sat near the opposite door as heavily as a sulky spouse. It occupied all of the back seat, like a family of strange, muted children. And it brushed at the back of your neck to make it bristle like the hair of a hostile cat.

This thing had tentacles that broke off to become worms, and they crawled everywhere, sucking the air from your lungs and putting kettle drums in your ears where a thunderous solo marked your heartbeat.

There was the impression of a grin somewhere in the car, an amused grin that marked a perverse satisfaction, and it lingered as the road climbed steadily up the side of the valley, sometimes brushing so close to the trees that it was like passing through a roadless woods.

The sense of the "something" became so strong that it threatened to take over the driving, for what could only be disaster—a plunge over the embankment and a drop into the black abyss, or a collision with a gnarled tree.

It was not a time to apply reason. That would have been as offensive and impossible as becoming suddenly clinical about love in a moment of passion. So this "something" rode along as the road ascended the steep hill, and just before the crest, where a switchback dictated a crawling speed, the aloneness returned with concussive force, and from somewhere down in the darkness of the valley, there was the sound of laughter so hollow that it produced sympathetic vibrations in your ribs.

Then it was over, and the cold sweat was there like the price of escape from a body bag or the clamminess of plastic underwear.

You say it never happened: I say it happened, and I've got proof. Though it occurred years ago, the hair on the back of my neck is still not totally relaxed.

NOVEMBER BONES

Now in November, you can see things to the bone. There is a sadness in that, a disappointment in viewing the unadorned framework of the land—skeleton trees, lifeless fields, vacant marshes. If April marks the passage of time with renewal, November does it more effectively by displaying the sprawling corpse of yet another season. It lies in state in glorious disorder, and the grand denial becomes increasingly difficult. The brutal truth is that it is only the duration of our life-span that separates us from the fallen leaves and the brittle weeds. It is impossible to refute this in November, when the days are as gray as mourning and the great chill creeps toward us from the polar ice cap.

It is our burden of intelligence that does it to us. We cannot take November at face value, as simply the beginning of the winter pause. Instead, we saddle it with emotional chores, and it throws us into a funk as certainly as it chases the geese and puts the bears to sleep. The ever-decreasing daylight spawns a dread that the final darkness approaches, and before it nothing is so vulnerable as man.

The cure for such depressing reverie may lie in the cause. If our burdensome ability to reason makes a personal doldrums of November, can't we step beyond such an egotistical interpretation to celebrate our presence at this time and this place? In the bare-bones assessment thrust upon us by this eleventh month, there are positive things to note. Things like pine cones and acorns—little packages of promise. Buck deer with lust-swollen necks, their genes safely stored in incubating wombs. And those sleeping bears, as fat as pigs and as certain of spring arousal as the return of the geese.

In these and a thousand other things is written the assurance of continuation. It is required reading now, as the current of time sweeps us downstream and another gray vortex extends a mocking invitation to the ominous party.

Now is the time to RSVP with authoritative regrets, to say "no" to the spiritual parasites that lurk in November. Kicking leaves on a wooded trail on a brisk afternoon will do it. So will pausing to watch a sunset, when the clouds become a spectacle of pink and lavender. Even watching the sleek, fat squirrel in the back yard can serve the purpose. From such simple activity must be drawn the forceful conclusions: I see, therefore I am. I appreciate, therefore I am man. It is November, and I am here as part of all of it, no more important than anything else but no less important, either.

THERE IN THE DAWN

The woods is full of strangeness now. In the low, gray days of late autumn, something inexplicable lurks in the moist pungency along the game trails, something as elemental as the swollen necks of rutting deer, and as ageless as the cycle of trees growing from the degeneration of their predecessors.

It is that biologic remnant from a time when the chilled earth began its Olympian selection process, and it stirs in our blood like a spirochete, uncoiling annually to produce arterial itches.

It is the autumnal assertion of our predator identity, and now the hunters stand in solitary darkness, waiting for the dawn with the strangeness all about them and within them, and with their hearts beating to a cadence older than glaciers.

The hunters have stepped from the portals of a velvet society, their hair clipped, their nails trimmed and their biologic instincts as processed and packaged as psychological wieners. They represent the cutting edge of the great confusion about killing, and while they respond to basic instincts that they cannot articulate, they become the targets of the self-righteous and the hypocritical.

The first light is as tentative as early smoke. There is only a subtle shifting in the blackness, and the hunter squirms in his blindness like an insect in the throes of metamorphic preparations.

Then, perhaps, he knows within himself the personal dichotomy, the outrageousness and the rightness of what he is doing; and something moves up his spine with the primordial wiggling energy of a spawning trout.

There is a rustling in the shadows—a noise of

movement, of some life form sharing the dawn; and the hunter feels the tensing and coiling and contracting that is older than any part of him. Then he is old with it, as old as the hairy, grunting ancestors who waited in other dawns.

The approaching day hesitates, retreats even, and while he inclines and strains slightly toward the sound, the hunter's eyes probe the ragged remains of night like the flicking tongue of a cobra.

There it is! A formless object disengaged from its inert surroundings—a thing of motion, of life, of prey. The light is not good, however, and there is no defining what is our "there," no way to tell with certainty its contours or its size.

But in the dimness of the dawn, the bonds have formed and solidified, until there is the hunter and there is the prey, attached to one another by an unbreakable umbilical of evolution. One waits to kill, the other to die. It is as preordained as tomorrow's sunrise, and it is the great tournament of survival that brought us out of the caves and to this point.

The form takes shape, animal shape, with a head and a neck and a body; and the hunter raises his weapon and begins to aim, seeing over the tube of cold steel the path of the projectile that he will send on its deadly mission.

It is the great coiling before the leap, the final lunge in the chase, the hissing stoop with talons extended. The hunter is consumed by it now, and he functions with the mindless focus of a killer cell. He is not a rational being acting out a role that is no more essential to his existence than the ability to climb trees: At this second, he is an animal of the ages, no more and no less than the thousands of thick-browed hunter-fathers before him.

And then the twitch of his trigger finger changes it all. In the thunderous reverberations echoing through the trees, the ancient psyche crumbles to dust, and the hunter is left to contemplate his place in this rising day. He stands as a man of the moment, the lethal weapon heavy in his hands, and a life ending at his feet. In the name of biologic ancestors, he has killed as a "sport hunter." He cannot explain to you the depth and subtleties of that identity—particularly the way it seems to permit him to violate his own reverence for life, and how it makes it impossible for him to describe hunting in the stultifying terms of "fun" and "games."

This much is certain, however: During a brief dawn, the hunter was a player in the natural scheme of things, as unfettered and unencumbered in that role as his kind can get.

OLD DOGS

Winter was headed for the forest preserve like an eager surgical team, an impending swirl of white that would excise all but the bones. There was, in the waiting, a forlorn excitment. And in the solitude among the barren trees, you could shop for a seasonal or a personal prognosis.

The old man's walk was slow, almost a shuffle, and he came into view as an apparition of the season, as if he were emerging from the starkness all about with appropriate qualifications to take charge of this time of collapse and endings.

Then you could see the dog at his side, a very old dog with a muzzle as gray as mold, and long, shaggy hair that hung as spent and lifeless as the brown leaves of the oak overhead. The dog walked with stiff, measured steps, like a mechanical toy moving on the ebbing strength of a weakened spring. It looked neither right nor left, and after a time it became obvious that the worn old dog was either blind or so incredibly weary of its canine life that it did not want to see any more.

The old man was dressed in heavy clothing: a woolen coat, a hat that pulled down over his ears and the back of his neck, and thick mittens that encased his hands. It was sensible dress for the cold day, and the man wore it with the quiet authority and assurance that comes with long winters of experience.

Over its scraggly coat, the dog wore a faded blanket that buckled under its chest and hung down along its sides like a rug. It did not make the dog look silly, as some anthropomorphic pet costuming does. Instead, it gave the old animal a peculiar majesty, as if it were too old and smart to be out in the cold wind with just its worn pelt for protection.

A leather leash connected the man and the dog, but it was as slack as an old clothesline. It was as apparent as the chill in the December wind that their bonds lay in the slow synchronization of their movement, choreographed and rehearsed to perfection by companionship and time.

They walked the edge of the parking area, past a sign that said "no dogs allowed" and past one of those low-slung cars that symbolizes a society that sometimes says "no old allowed." They did not look at the occasional passerby, and if there was any communication between them, it was as silent as thought.

At the end of the parking lot, they made the turn and headed back with the wind, their slow, deliberate pace a modest display of monumental dignity. And on this occasion of harsh seasonal reminders about the cyclic nature of all things, they made a powerful statement about accepting personal winters with ultimate grace.

At their car, the dog stood patiently and still, while the man removed his mittens and unlocked the vehicle's doors. Then the old man bent slowly and laboriously to lift the dog gently onto the back seat. They left then, both of them in their respective car seats, looking straight ahead, as sober as surgeons and with their stiffening old spines as defiant of winter's approach as the leafless trees.

60,000 BEAKS

It was the day the geese went south. It was a magnificent spectacle in the gray skies over the Midwest, and to witness it was to be awed anew at the strength and magnitude of natural cycles.

The great birds came by the thousands in wavering V's and ragged lines. They were a half-mile high, riding a tailwind out of the north and sliding along beneath a cloud ceiling that hands December over like a smothering mother.

They filled the sky, strange and delicate chorus lines performing a number as old as feathers.

This was no random flight by feeding birds that wear out their welcome in suburban back yards and city parks. This was the vanguard of the wild flyway flock that lives more to its own beat and less to the drum of civilization.

The birds' cries came down to the brown and sodden earth faintly, like the yelps of demented children playing in the clouds. The sound came to your ears with genetic baggage, and you knew that you had heard it before, 10,000 years ago.

Earlier in the day, the geese had left central Wisconsin. First they massed in swirling, twisting, babbling flocks over marshes and fields; then slowly out of the birdy bedlam, a structure evolved. The V's and lines formed and reformed, and then by a signal mysteriously produced in the atmosphere and the tilt of the earth, some 60,000 Canada geese pointed their beaks south and began the long trip.

The birds' strong wings began the rhythmic pumping that would go on steadily for nine or ten hours as the geese made the 400- to 500-mile nonstop trip to refuges where Illinois, Missouri, and Kentucky come together in a twist of river-dictated boundaries.

Thousands of others would follow in the days to come, but this day was the big one. It was like a celebration in the sky. From a single point along its route, it went on for several hours. It seemed to have no beginning and no end, and there was a feeling that it might go on forever.

It was, by all counts, the greatest show on earth on a recent cloudy December day, and the tragedy of it is that so many people missed it, busy as they were traveling in seasonal cycles of their own.

But if you saw the show, it stirred the biological soup in your makeup and did something to your spirit. Some small part of you went south with the great birds, flying among the majestic flocks like a sparrow—aimless, yet directed beyond all doubt.

GET OUT OR GET READY

There is an implicit threat across the wild land now. It is there in the short, gray days where it borders on the sinister. It dominates the long, dark nights with the dispassion and patience of a hit squad. It says this: Get out or get ready. This is the beginning of the annual shakeout, when the cycle of life ebbs lowest and corpses of the "old" seed a million new cellular crops. Get out or get ready.

The message is clarion-clear to the slow and the dumb. Great snapping turtles with marble-sized brains bury themselves in primordial muck, there to exist like metamorphic boulders beneath the ice and water.

Furry creatures, as single-purposed as sperm, gorge themselves to obesity, then crawl away to sleep the sleep that flirts with death. They occupy caves and burrows and depressions under tree roots and windfalls, temporary and dark places like those where the ancestors of man once sought shelter from the dangerous resonance of the message. Only a blink of time separates these tenant classes of the dark places, and that fact is somehow part of the message now.

Birds—millions and millions of birds—receive the message in mysterious receptors designed by the ages; they "get out" in a twittering, honking movement that is at once awesomely organized and incredibly chaotic. The Canada goose is the designated announcer for the migration, but its cries come untranslated and garbled to flightless listeners. There is something in the cries, something that buzzes like a mosquito in a sensory vacuum, but its meaning remains forever just out of reach.

High over a swamp, against a sky as gray as mourning, a lone eagle soars. It cuts lazy circles over the thick brush and grass, and it holds its position above the decomposing carcass of a deer that had been shot during the recent deer season. The eagle had drifted down from the north, responding as certainly as the geese to the message of the season, and now it rests on the wind as it contemplates the means of surviving for another day.

But it sails away toward the south until it is out of sight, perhaps drawn by the message and perhaps refusing to share the swamp with anything but the dead deer.

Maybe it will come back. If not, other scavengers will dispose of the deer. The carcass will sustain the likes of coyote and fox and a flock of raucous crows, all species that shun the "get out or get ready" message. The scavengers will struggle for survival with each gray day. This they have in common with man, whose brain has grown so large that he need not acknowledge the message and, in fact, can no longer really comprehend it.

For that reason, man's role in the natural scheme of things must be suspect. And suspicion must also mount over the positioning of a species that has the technology to kill a deer but lacks the capacity to find it after it is dead.

These are the questions for gray days, when the message to get out or get ready is on the cold wind, like a whisper from some other place.

Goodnight, Sweet Bears

It is time to put the wild bears to bed, to wander the trails of the northwoods, where the great black beasts reign like bishops, and where skeletal trees sway to the rising moan of ice-age ghosts. The bears go to their winter sleep now as the impassively condemned, sauntering to temporary graves. They inter themselves as biologic pilgrims, never knowing, never doubting that on the other side of the darkness of their transient tombs is a bear's salvation.

Something of that is over the wild land, a subliminal decree as elemental to survival as thirst and hunger. You can feel it in the retreat of the sun in the late afternoon, when the shadows of glacial-tumbled boulders shift and shrug like perched scavengers; and it is there along the edges of the thickest spruce swamps, where there is always an oozing of the eternal night.

From the highest hill in the sylvan land of bears, the panorama filtering through the barren trees gives the impression of abandonment, of all life having somehow partied with summer and then sneaked off to avoid responsibility. But that is a false assessment, born of arrogance and ignorance: only the opportunists defect when the leaves fall; only the gaudy and the noisy depart when the wind bites; and only a fool concludes that a land is lifeless when it sustains such entities as bears.

On a park sign designating the start of a wilderness trail, big slivers of wood have been gnawed off the neatly lettered boards. The puncture marks of large fangs identify the woodworker as a bear, and the damage to the sign leaves little doubt as to the power of the jaws behind the fangs. It is difficult to avoid the anthropomorphic temptation to credit the bear with trying to say something to sign makers or sign readers. The recent incident of bears killing a man in a western park comes to mind. So does the fact that here in these wild tracts, a bear hunting season has just ended, in which several hundred bears were chased by dogs or lured into bait before being shot.

But a bear is too dumb for all but instinctive anger. It is too dumb to hold grudges, to plot revenge, to use mechanical aids such as guns in its adversarial relationship with us. It can only obey the basic urges to eat and to rest and to protect its young, and then one day in the late fall to find a hiding place for its annual rendezvous with the little death.

For this, it warrants utter respect from anyone who would come into its land for purposes of synchronizing psyche and season, or to excise burdens of the spirit caused by too many headlines about child-killing and children-starving and global inhumanity to man.

The trail twists into the thick balsam and spruce, where the green moss is like a water-soaked mattress. On an emerald-colored log, the gnawed remains of a deer antler lie like a stored dose of calcium for the red squirrels. On a hardwood ridge between the swamps, the dried scat of a coyote is white against the leaves. It is made of deer hair and slivers of bone, and its message is as plain as a discarded soup can.

Then, on the shady side of a towering mound of glacial debris, as the trail swings back toward the swamps, there is something different in the cold whisper of the wind. Perhaps, as with all things, the difference is only in the perception, but a stillness emanates up from the thick leaf cover and puts the wind to rest. Suddenly then there is the unmistakable sound of wood breaking, the sustained cracking of a sizable branch or stump being fractured and splintered. It is the noise a bear might make as it searched nearby for one last grub, or perhaps sought to punctuate another sign.

Quiet follows. It is brittle quiet. It goes on, and then finally the wind picks up where it had left off, forlorn sighs in the topmost branches.

So the imagination and the perverse mental baggage and the wildness of the remote setting and the simple, eloquent language of the bear set up a cacophony. It is ferocious and loud, the unrestrained, howling yawn of the universe.

Certainly then, the bears—all of them—meander closer to their beds, and mortal guests depart on tip-toe, stepping lively, of course.

Winter

THE WATER IS US

Now is the time of settling in, when the northern hemisphere tilts into cold shade and life forms scurry like parasites on a cooling corpse. It is the annual humbling, and as the elemental order of things is asserted, the ego becomes dangerous baggage.

Somewhere beneath the strata of the millenniums that brought us to this point, there developed a primitive survival twitch that has clung, leech-like, to our being. It squirms within us now, generating signals our system can no longer decode.

In this season of pondering and pontificating, it is appropriate to offer outrageous speculation about such things, to leap like a cricket into deep philosophic ponds, where great minds swim as barracuda.

We consider then the evolutionary parade that came slithering out of the brine as fiddler crabs played "Won't You Come Home, Bill Bailey," and black muck hid the numberless forks in the Yellow Brick Road. So we are up from water, and it is water that we are largely comprised of, and it is water that sustains us. And now, at this reduced angle to the sun, this fundamental ingredient of our being becomes something else, something unyielding that discombobulates the warm cycles of life that embrace us.

On a frigid morning, clouds of vaporous water hang over the tall buildings of the city, rolling slowly up into a blue sky as the cold ghosts of great fires, then dissolving like memory. It is the discarded water of heating systems that preserve vulnerable human life, and it evaporates back into grand natural storage, along with the exhaled breath of the scurrying masses. In its endless recycling, there is no hint of this water's indifference, that it served the lungs of primordial predecessors with similar dispatch, and that it has been here before as mountainous glaciers.

Over the flowing streams now, there is a war for possession of surface water. It is fought between the plummeting temperature of the air and the eddying currents of the rivers and creeks. You can see its writhing and agony in the vapor that twists up on cold days, like the dancing of a million ethereal weasels. Slowly, as the winter deepens and the air slides out of the north with cumulative arctic authority, the streams lose, and the flowing water is replaced by ice as hard and lifeless as concrete.

The lakes and the ponds are similarly covered. At the beaches, blankets of snow are spread, and crumbs of ice are scattered by moaning ghostly picnickers that come with the north wind. Along the wild shores, cattails rattle like the scabbarded swords of a disintegrating army, and the domes of muskrat houses look as dead as graves. In these places, where the summer wind and sun combine to produce sensory symphonies that soothe our innermost beasts, there is nothing now but the hardness and the cold.

We are vaguely uncomfortable with that. It goes deeper than some of the more recent evolutionary developments when we bet our intelligence against instinct and wait now for the next card. This is more elemental. The cold of the season has taken away easy access to the omnipotent mother of all life, the one so basic that we forget her with the complacency of suckling babes.

Once we were on the same road with the turtle who sleeps away this season in the warm water beneath the ice. Who is to say that we did not make the wrong turn?

Therein is the old twitch.

THE SEASON OF SHORT DAYS

We come now to the season of short days, when darkness and cold wither all things and the spirit begins its evasive scurry. From deep within us, our id seeks the protection of light, gathering and hoarding all that is available, like an opportunistic squirrel, stuffing the waning brightness into recesses of the moment.

In the woods, the day begins with a breathless hush, as if somewhere in the darkness a baton had been raised and all attention drawn to an omniscient conductor. There is not so much an advance of day as there is a retreat of night, a subtle slippage and rearranging of the blackest shadows as they shift down off the hardwood ridges and gather in the coniferous thickets, where they will huddle all day like brooding owls.

An innocuous little tick or scratch or chirp triggers the day, like the first tiny crack in fresh, black ice; it signals the crows to begin their patrols. They claim the day like cops, asserting authority as if they had been anointed and surveying the ravages of the night with an aerial swagger.

Then the other birds are there: geese marching overhead to a crying cadence, woodpeckers discussing bugs in tapping codes, and chickadees doing their butterfly flutters from twig to twig.

The sun is a bloody eye that peeks over the jagged horizon with cold boredom, and before its unblinking stare, all those players with roles in the brief day assume their places. Squirrels shuffle and sort through the gathering light and the fallen leaves to put meat on their bones, preparing themselves for the predators that will come to devour them during the season of short days.

Deer finish their early morning feeding and curl in hidden beds to masticate at each other in mute lectures of rumination. Hawks turn their fierce concentration to the business at hand, and soar over the new day with the license of executioners in their needle talons.

The day wind bestirs itself and sighs to activity, sometimes building to a leaf-rattling bluster and sometimes giving in to a sun-bathed stillness that is like a paralysis, as if an ancient voice had rumbled up from the depths of the earth with dire reminders about ice-age cycles.

And then the short day becomes a prolonged ending. Even before it has really begun, it gets itself all tangled up in long shadows and hazy clouds, and the light begins to cower. To stay with it then, tuned intimately to the circadian cycle, is to feel the great ebbing in all of your senses—the reassertion of the night stillness, the return of the chill, and the slow blindness that comes like a strange, dark fog.

It ends frequently in a spectacular sunset, when the sky is fired by flaming clouds and bruised with a pink and lavender beauty that flares and then fades; then there is nothing to see but the march of the stark tree silhouettes passing into darkness and beyond.

The short days now are glancing blows from a sun on an ever-lowering arc, and they come as taunts to the diurnal creatures. These brief periods of daylight are all we will get now for months to come. And since we have given the evolutionary cold shoulder to behavioral patterns that would give us relief from such a seasonal pattern, it is ours to suffer the short days in grim silence, mining them for nuggets of daylight like eccentric hermits; and hoping to God we can keep our spirits from descending into their own long, dark nights.

AS THE CROW FLIES

In the first half-light, crows spill out of their spruce roost like the ripened fruit of the night. They sail off on silent wings, the darkness of the season compressed in their blackness, and the futility of complaining about short days in their monotone squawks.

The crows' decisions are the first of the day in the neighborhood, made in the freedom that comes only with the undomesticated life—no jobs, no transportation schedules, no timetables imposed by bureaucrats, bosses, or social structures. Just the simple yet incredibly complicated job of getting safely through the day and fueling the metabolic system.

So, where to fly? And never mind the "how" of it when the big breast muscles pull the wings down against the resistance of turbulent air, and the take-offs and landings are precise and perfect. This miraculous behavior is made unalterably flawless by the bird's split-second decisions, and therefore we regard it as commonplace and unworthy of consideration, though we have never contemplated the challenge of dealing with gravity, wind, and aerodynamics in coming out of flight to perch in the top of a wind-whipped tree.

It is instinctive, mechanical behavior, of course, but still the bird's brain is involved; and by comparison, decisions about which train to catch or when to change traffic lanes are as dull as scratching.

On this tentative day, then, as the crow files a flight plan with its stomach, it heads toward the dumpster in back of the fast food store, where the scraps of hamburgers and fries are sometimes spilled on the asphalt. It has been a good place before, but during the night the rats have cleaned it with the thoroughness of surgical janitors, and there isn't enough left to feed a sparrow.

There are always the road kills—a gray squirrel, perhaps, that lies near the curb and would make a high protein breakfast. But there are not enough gaps in the endless traffic that hisses past inches away from the dead squirrel; the crow can only perch and look, like a shopper when the stores are closed.

Maybe it is a day to go to the country, to gain some altitude and fly over the suburban maze to the cornfields where the pickings are always good—golden kernels of corn spilled everywhere—and where a crow can relax in the sun-washed treetops like a vacationer. But the wind is wrong, and it is a long flight, and there must be something easier to get.

On one such day, a crow landed high in a bare oak and went about eating its breakfast which, with the aid of binoculars, was identified as a bluegill. The crow does not fish, and anyway it was miles from the nearest lake. Where would it get a bluegill?

Crows are like that, opportunists of the highest order, adapting like feathers in the wind, and the workings of their brains are ever more mysterious. How do they make decisions to fly where they do? What is the thought process whereby a crow goes to the neighborhoods where the garbage is out for collection, or sometimes flies higher than seems necessary to get from here to there?

Crows are not required for this kind of contemplative jump rope. Sparrows will do. Or chickadees. How is it that the trio of chickadees visits the feeder at 3:15 in the afternoon? Where have the tiny birds been all day, and did one of them or all three of them participate in the decision to flutter out of the shrubbery and make their restless collection of seeds at the backyard smorgasbord? And how can a brain so tiny make the decisions necessary to survive the rigors of a northern winter?

So now, as winter approaches with the authority of a brass band, these birdy questions occupy the mind to the exclusion of more appropriate inquiry, i.e. if we are the smartest, why don't we migrate to a warmer place? Or perhaps crawl into bed and sleep until March?

But then we are involved in so much obtuse behavior that if we start any meaningful introspection, we would probably self-destruct. It is much easier to wonder how the crow avoids crash landings, and how one of them once ended up with a bluegill breakfast.

THE SCREAM

Something patrolled along the creek in the night. Something supple and solitary came undulating over the deep white snow with the soft tread of a nocturnal sorcerer, its tracks a careless suturing beside the black wound of the stream.

It dragged its belly here and there as it snooped beside the slick waters, and occasionally it slipped down to inspect the cold filigree on the thin edge of forming ice.

It was all the discarded script of a wild mink, put down with careless precision after a single performance, and infinitely taunting to an audience that is forever tardy.

Then, from beneath the festering of memory like a seed of malignancy, came the piercing echoes of an old animal scream. It was anthropomorphised, more now than originally, into a horrible screech of anger and outrage; and again it came with an ice-pick agony to the ears and rode an obscene shock wave out across the tranquillity of the wild land.

The mink's original scream had come as it struggled in the indescribable cruelty of a steel trap, and as its impending doom loomed over it in the form of the stick-wielding boy whose conscience was pitifully embryonic.

That scream, benign these decades and never interfering with the mundane daily flow of things, had metastasized now to poison it all. It hung in the cold day as lethal vapors, and it glistened in the spray of water from the wings of the startled mallards, as they leaped into the air and pumped desperately to clear the alder brush and the jack pine.

It faded some when a small flock of chickadees and nuthatches fluttered about suddenly, the tiny birds alighting within arm's reach and bobbing off to better company, their calls like harmless gossip in the quiet of the woods.

Then, as the creek winds along the bottom of the ridge where the bedroom of the deer is one great, white mattress and the animals' tracks poke into it like the marks of sticks, the awful old echo was as faint as a zephyr. The explosive flush of grouse from beneath a juniper erased it, finally, then there was the magnificent quiet, a balm as healing as Morpheus.

There are times when the inclination to seek refuge comes to the psyche as a storm, when catastrophic events and convoluted circumstance rage beyond the capacity to endure. Then, for the emotionally wounded and the morally dispossessed, the wild land is a place where ultimate harmony is woven from the variegated threads of natural law, and it becomes a cloak over sagging shoulders.

But the fit is never good. No matter the shrugging and the tugging, the natural symmetry cannot accommodate the outrageousness of greed and cruelty, the absurdity of prejudice and hate, and the boundless capacity for destruction and bloodshed.

The exercise of this despicable behavior across species lines is one thing: As abused as it is in this context, its obdurate character may hang its hat on the laws of survival.

But what sometimes makes such moral corruption particularly galling is its extravagant display within the species that is most advanced and intelligent, and within which we are all as torturously trapped as the helpless mink of long ago.

And so we know the scream, and it lies in our throats like bile.

The Dead Duck

The story of how the tiny duck died was written in the ice around it. It told of an ever-decreasing area of open water, until finally the brutal cold closed in and sealed the bird into the steel-hard ice of the creek.

Sometime during the night, the cold had invaded the duck's body like an infestation of minute, murderous parasites. It had crawled through the feathers, the down, and the skin, and into the flesh, where the exquisite arrangement of organs and fluids made the bird a miraculous product of the eons.

At some point, the duck had bowed to it, dipping its head low where it froze in a submissive tilt, as its blood congealed and its heart stopped beating.

We found it that way the next day, as we skated up the twisting channel. There were three or four of us, prepubescent boys with red cheeks and damp noses, and the discovery of the duck stopped our exuberant exploration.

We stood on wavering ankles and stared down at the bird, our breaths forming a cluster of miniature clouds and our eyeballs threatening to roll from our heads. Nobody spoke for a second or two, then somebody muttered a boyish version of a curse in a whispery voice. We knelt around it, our bony knees and elbows down on the ice, and tried to look the dead duck in the eye.

"Maybe it's not dead yet," somebody said.

We wanted that to be true. We were too full of life, too much on the brink of living, too engrossed in the grand potential of a lifetime to give any consideration to death. We could not, in fact, even manage a remote grasp of it.

But here it was, in front of us as certainly as the dried

bird nest in the willow thicket and the mink tracks through the cattails. The resistance went on, however; somebody suggested we get a hatchet and chop the duck out of the ice and take it to somebody's home, where it might thaw out and come back to life.

One of us touched the duck's head with a mittened hand; it was as solid as a baseball. We all touched it then, like timid worshipers at a strange shrine.

"Why didn't it go south?" somebody asked.

"Maybe it was wounded by a hunter and couldn't fly," someone else said.

The cold from the ice crept into our elbows and our knees as we knelt there, and then the connection was somehow made. The cold had killed the duck. The frigid temperature that had come slinking in from the north suddenly took on villainous dimensions, and a kind of horror frost was formed in our boyish brains. The brutal, duck-killing cold would not get back into our warm homes.

We skated away then, slowly and subdued. And we went to our respective homes early, even before the short winter day creaked to a dark, bone-chilling end.

Then the other day, when the awful cold descended and caressed us all with its life-sucking tentacles, the frozen duck was there again, and I realized that I had been seeing it off and on over the years. The image does not fade; instead, it seems more vivid each time it appears.

WHAT THE CHRISTMAS TREE WAS

A little piece of the woods occupies a corner in most homes this time of year, but the connection with nature that the Christmas tree provides is often lost in the hustle and glitz of the holidays.

Sometimes, however, the scent of balsam, pine, or spruce dominates even the aroma of baking cookies or roasting turkey. Then, if you grab a moment away from the wrapping and unwrapping, you can contemplate the tree for what it was before it came to your home for its moment of festooned glory.

It was, of course, a living thing, a cellular maze with roots reaching into the earth like groping tentacles and needle-laden branches combing sustenance out of the sunshine.

It was a cone-shaped cog in a highly integrated community, whether it grew in a plantation row or a random clearing among the hardwood. Its natural destiny should have given it decades, but its life-span was determined by the tree grower's bottom line, and it fell to a saw as unceremoniously as a stalk of grain.

Most of the trees grow in the north country, on the edge of that vast area of dark, mysterious winters where wild things howl with the moaning wind and yellow-eyed owls, as white and silent as ghosts, glide over the drifted snows.

If you look deep into the shadowy depths of your Christmas tree, where the thickest branches meet the trunk, you can imagine these kinds of things. You can recall the tree's seasons:

Those winters, always the winters, so cold sometimes that tree trunks exploded in contracting contortions, and malnourished deer curled up on snowy trails and died.

Those springs, when the frost let go of the tree's roots and the first warm breeze brushed its needles. Then the land came alive around it, and it was trimmed with the sounds of a million creatures. Delicate flowers grew at its feet, and strange yodels echoed down from migrating cranes.

Those summers, when the sandy hillside or the rocky valley where it grew was alive with birdsong and shaken by thunderous storms. When it was bigger, it was sometimes selected as a nesting site by a pair of cardinals or blue jays, and then its summer was a special time as it contributed to the reproduction of a different life form.

Those autumns—when they came, it was always another foot taller, sometimes more than that, and the new growth that clung to it was the magnificent decoration of the annual cycle. It could never be trimmed more beautifully, and it stood straight and sturdy, as the maples turned blood red and the aspen dropped gold leaves to the earth.

However farm-like and organized its growth might have been, it was a thing of wildness, an evergreen plant descended from great forests that sprouted centuries ago in the outwash of towering glaciers. You can feel that kind of history in the sharpness of its needles, or sense it in its woodsy pungency.

You can also know your own history better if, when no one else is around, you crouch low in front of the tree, perhaps even lie down under it. Then, as you gaze up into the decorations and the shadows, the memories of your childhood descend on you like a warm shower.

Our own cycles are inextricably entwined with the Christmas trees in our lives. But unlike the nesting birds that only came to use it for a while, we are the ultimate consumers, and now the tree's life is over.

Next year there will be another tree, and if we are lucky we will be around to consider the tree's life cycle as it gift-wraps our own.

THE HAWK, THE MOUSE,
AND THE MUSKRAT

The December fog was there in the morning, like the cold dust of night. It blurred the vision of all eyes, reducing individual worlds to gray cocoons.

The horizon was fringed by bare-limbed trees, frozen in groping postures that had been fashioned by the hot days of past summers.

The slowly swirling fog was a tradeoff for the woods creatures, providing a thin screen for those whose lives hang by sight-line threads and presenting a minor inconvenience to the predators—perhaps a delay of only seconds in the swoop and crunch that means death and breakfast.

A goshawk, bomb-shaped and as still as a decoy, perched on the limb of a fog-shrouded oak. It watched the marsh with the stern countenance of an executioner, and it dared any living thing to move within the sweep of its piercing eyes.

The marsh was graveyard-still, but beneath the surface there was abundant life. A ragged mound of broken rushes and mud protruded out of the marsh ice like a big worn-out ball. Within its hollow center, a muskrat napped in the kind of security that is rare to rodent species.

In a hundred solitary nooks, mice gnawed at dried vegetation and seeds, their bright beady eyes like tiny black pearls. Then, for reasons known only to it, one of the mice decided to move to another cluster of rushes. It poked its nose out first, testing the air in the vigilance that was its only life insurance.

The mouse's field of vision did not include the hawk; so it began its move, a darting scamper to the next bog.

The hawk's muscles tensed, and it was airborne in a fraction of a second. Its broad wings sliced through the cold fog like feathered knives as the bird used gravity and subtle shifts of its body to accelerate its slanting descent.

The hawk and the mouse arrived at the bog together—the mouse leaping frantically, and the hawk tilting its wings abruptly and extending its curved, needle-like talons. There was a writhing mass of shadowy movement and a whoosh of cold, morning air.

The hawk's breakfast problem had been solved. So had the mouse's.

In its house, the muskrat slept on. Someday, after another marsh drama when a trapper comes this way, the muskrat's shiny coat might get it a ride to the city in a fancy car.

Chains of one kind or another bind all life forms to the marsh. Some of the links seem strange, like the coat in the car, but on this foggy December morning, the hawk and the mouse came together as naturally as lovers.

CROWBAIT

Crows come flying silently down out of the winter fog. They glide easily, dipping their wings only slightly, like carrion birds coming to a corpse. They swerve in the damp, gray air and clutch at the topmost branches of the oak trees with their scaly black claws. Then they perch way up there with their neckless, Ed Sullivan profiles stark against the sodden sky, and their beady black diamond eyes see everything.

They sit there, thinking thoughts as plain on their shiny feathers as the droplets of mist that seem to fall upward from the slush-covered earth.

No thoughts of the past and no thoughts of the future. No regrets, no plans. Only bird-brain thoughts for this cold, damp moment and what it offers.

It offers a crow this: bread crusts around the garbage can, the companionship of other crows, an acorn for lunch, perhaps an owl to taunt, a dog to watch, a place to perch, and a time to preen.

The crow is dumb. Its brain is smaller than a golf ball, and it cannot know that if yesterday was worse, tomorrow might be better. It doesn't even know that it will roost in the pine trees tonight and find breakfast tomorrow, but it will—without planning and without worrying.

Other crows come, until there is a convention of preeners clinging to the very tips of the treetops. They do not look through the window where I sit beneath the glow of a light bulb and stare out at them. The big black birds don't care, and it doesn't matter to them whether I watch.

Then I take my eyes away for a second, and when I look back they are gone. But not really. Their images roost on a branch of memory. And then I think: The crows would find me interesting only if I were dead. Maybe they just come around once in a while to see how I'm doing.

You have to like a creature that lives for the moment and sees you only in terms of crowbait.

THE JANUARY MOON

There was something special about the January moon that now wanes away to the incessant nibbling of time. Maybe it was special because it presided over a series of winter nights when the temperature was mild and pleasant, instead of brutally cold.

That blunting of the annual period of long, cold nights gave the moon a quality of friendliness. There was, in its brightness, a reminder that it is the same heavenly body that turns lovers' brains into pancake batter in the spring and makes blathering romantics of old men in the autumn.

It was the kind of unusual winter moon that invited you out on a date and dared you to refuse lest you miss a rare opportunity.

It happened on a night when the moon was full, riding over the wooded hills like the wheel of a great chariot spun off during a race beyond our comprehension.

It was in the country, far from traffic and streetlights, and the silence of the night was magnificent accompaniment to the splendor of the moon. There was the kind of quiet that is virtually unknown to modern society—no background buzzing, no distant traffic roar, no jets, nothing but the flawless, ringing quiet of the woods and fields.

The moon washed out the stars, and only the brightest of them shown against a blue-steel sky. The moonlight spilled down over the tree limbs that stretched across the country road, and shadows on the icy road surface were like huge spider webs.

The snow-covered hills crawled with more shadows, so thick and so blended as to tangle your perception. Then sometimes the immobility of it all became a sea of subtle movement, like a mysterious tide running across the land in response to the pull of the moon.

The air was so fresh and pure that it was like a stimulant. There can be no argument: Inhaling January moonlight brings a high beyond that of the most powerful drug. The function of breathing was elevated from the base of the brain to the conscious levels, where pleasure and sensory joy are noted.

The road bent around the base of a thickly wooded hill, and the musical tinkle of a small stream came into the silence of the night like the whispered secrets of children. From the railing of the bridge, you could listen to the beauty of the sound, the same through the eons and yet different every second.

Then you could feel the peace and quiet of the countryside, and some of the moonlight seemed to soak into your bones to produce a warmth that went far beyond anything like the burning of calories.

And there, on that bridge on the country road, listening to the creek, with the shadows and the moonlight all about, there was a moment as grand as January can produce.

To miss such things is to wane like the moon.

The Sleepers

Now the woods are like a great bedroom, with various life forms snoozing away the cold days and the long nights. If you stand still in the middle of it all, you can imagine a gentle snoring. The great natural harmony is at rest, and it produces a subtle, symphonic sensation in your bones.

Millions of tiny hearts have slowed until their beat is as measured as the thumping of a death drum. Within the curled bodies of gophers, ground squirrels, and other sleepers, blood circulates only enough to sustain the spark of life—not enough to produce the electrical pulses necessary for brain function.

So the creatures sleep dumb, as senseless as balls of fur, and they play no part in the genetically programmed scheme that allows them to survive the time of cold and darkness.

Sometimes, when the weather warms, some of the sleepers rouse themselves. You can tell when the skunk takes a winter walk by the way it fills the night air with its special pungence.

The raccoon leaves its hand-like prints in the black mud along the creek banks when it leaves its hollow tree for a mid-winter snack.

And the possum ventures forth like something thrown together from spare parts. On a recent afternoon, one made its laborious way along a cluttered fence line, its bright, beady eyes belying the dullness of its mental faculties. It gave a snarling "grin" to the approach of another fence line walker, and its many needle-like teeth were as ominous-looking as the fangs of a dragon.

Farther north, bears sleep the winter away under

windfalls and stumps, and their somnolent survival program is even more finely tuned and complex, because it must allow for the birth of cubs. Tiny things that wouldn't fill a teacup emerge from the womb and grope blindly for the mammary glands that will keep them alive until the alarm clock of spring awakens their mother.

But birthing and such things aside, sleep prevails now across that part of the earth that is tilted sharply away from the sun. Private stores of fat fuel the countless idling engines of the sleeping creatures, and they wait in unconscious grace for better times.

Those of us who must stay awake through it all know spasms of envy that we do not recognize. We are related to the sleepers, but we cannot use their ways to weather the annual storm of darkness. Something deep within us regrets that.

However:

To sleep! Perchance to dream; ay, there's the rub;
For in that sleep of death what dreams may come.

Perhaps it is better to stay awake after all. There is no risk of bad dreams, and if we slept, we would miss the beauty of blizzards and the spirited cardinal that will start singing soon in the tops of the tallest trees.

THE VALLEYS

Now winter juggles our spirits in an agony of fumbling. But there are places where we can find shelter from the buffeting. There are the valleys.

The valley caught my eye in the twilight as I drove a rural road beside a winding stream. It was a valley of shadows, of darkness creeping down from the wooded hills, of the powerful somnolence of winter; and it pulled at my bones with a strange, velvet-gloved gravity.

It may have something to do with the marrow of our psyche being seasonally drawn back toward the fork in the evolutionary river that denied us hibernation. In any case, the valleys of wintry shadows beckon with the gnarled fingers of twisted time. So there was nothing to do but obey.

The cross-country skis slipped over the granulated snow to a hissing cadence that seemed to be whispered from some unseen point far up the valley. The motion was easy and rhythmic, and in the gathering darkness, there was the odd sensation that ties to the earth were being broken; that as the light continued to fade, the skis would lift off the snow, and in the darkness I would become one with the valley—an invisible element, dissolved by time and circumstance.

Clouds hid the stars, and as the day's last light seeped down into the snow, the valley took on a womb-like quality. Then you could use your imagination to deny your own existence and recalculate your position among the unborn of Mother Earth.

The valleys will do this kind of thing for you in the winter. Sometimes little touches of this will occur, even in the valleys of the city—those created by the architects and the builders. On rare occasions, something from the base relationship of winter and man will flash for a second from the side of a city "valley," and there will be a lurch of the psyche. Is the valley saying then to sleep the sleep until spring, or is it commanding a migration to a place where winter survival is easier?

No one knows the answer, of course, except that in a cellular kind of way, everyone knows.

The hissing of the skis stopped where the steep hill at the head of the valley loomed in the darkness like a great wall. There was a silence then, so deep and so profound that no living thing could have been a part of it. So, there in the valley on the doorstep of a long winter night, I ceased to exist.

That these words see the light of day is yet another strange quirk of such wintry times and sheltering places.

WHO, INDEED?

The winter nights wrap us now in a black embrace, bear-like in its smothering and frightening in its dominance. We scurry to escape it like rodents headed for the sanctuary of burrows, and beneath the glare of artificial light, we deny the night's embrace and tinker with our inner clocks as if they were as simple as egg timers.

They are not, of course, and sometimes their complexity is demonstrated in strange signals from things that dwell in dark places within us—inexplicable urges to go home, the unexpected desire to nap, a depth of sleep that summer never brings.

Conclusions come more easily than questions to the armchair anthropologist: Something is awry. Our present condition is one of those mistakes that nature pretends to make, only to correct it later with a biologic bang. In our hairless condition, we were not meant to survive icy, tempestuous winters, not without a period of hibernation.

We are saved from the inevitable alternative of protective hair or prolonged sleep by outsized brains that learned of fabrics and central heating systems.

But there is something tenuous, even phony, about this escape from the process of selectivity. It can be only temporary, and it can be only a matter of time before the "bang" swallows us in some kind of natural adjustment that we do not have the capacity to envision.

In the country now, where the winter night is not held at bay by electrical devices over huddled masses, there may emerge some vague sense of our condition. There is first the darkness; and sometimes beneath thick clouds, it can be as total as blindness, muted by the stars or the moon to allow the eyes to register the starkness of the winter landscape and to note that there are no other people about.

Then you can know the night with an intimacy reserved for lovers. It caresses with gentle zephyrs that seem to spring from the unseen undulating of the earth, and it whispers in a language that is spoken nowhere and understood everywhere.

To be alone with the winter night on the deserted prairie or in the silent woods is to feel its power and to know some little hint of its effect on all things. Then the quick conclusions about the warping of selectivity become the big personal question. It is posed with exquisite simplicity by the owl, that guardian and exploiter of the night. The quavering "Who, Who, Who?" is the transitional vehicle needed to reduce lofty philosophic meandering to a personal level that is more appropriate to our egocentricity.

Now, in the long hours of darkness, when nature is thwarted by technology and we must therefore stay awake, we are left to contemplate the owl's question.

Who, indeed?

The answer is somewhere out there in the winter night, as our inner clocks tick away the seconds and the lifetimes.

THE INTERSECTING CYCLES

Sometimes now in the dead of winter, the cycles intertwine and turn in on themselves, and we are caught in the tangled web of it all. Then biologic elitism becomes a sham, and we are alone with our conscience through the long, dark nights.

Old dog faces—tongues lolling and eyes bright—peer from the tangle of cycles. Their times are like empty beds by cooling hearths, where only gray dreams curl; and in their silent whines, they beg patiently for a scrap of meaning. Why were we here, and what was the significance of our being together, and where are we now?

Things killed, gentle creatures as dumb as sticks and birds as innocent as children, now all emerge from the vacuum of the past, and they stare from the back shadows of the cyclic jumble with expressions of offensive acceptance. No resentment. No "why." Just: This happened when our cycles intersected. Pigs, deer, chickens, quail. It is all the same.

Generations of chickadees, their cycle like a delicate necklace, visit the backyard bird feeder; and in their tiny, black-bead eyes there is nothing that says, "You have used your cycles to take our great forests and everything that we evolved to, and you have left us this, this little box of dry seeds."

Now a neighbor is gone, his cycle ending abruptly in his back yard when he went there with a chainsaw to get wood for his fire—a good, smiling man with grandchildren to enjoy and a wife to love. On the day he died, and the cars were around his house like metallic mourners, his gray-whiskered dog looked my way from the front yard, and the question hung between us: Why did his heart stop, and why does yours still beat? It was not posed by the dog— it was just there.

A great horned owl came one evening to sit in the tallest perch, where it could see in through the windows. It sat up there in the dead oak that clutches with rigor mortis limbs at a calloused sky. Appearance notwithstanding, the owl could not be given the anthropomorphic trappings of judgmental abilities. In the stillness of the cold, early twilight, it looked only to kill some small creature, to end a cycle so its own might continue. If the owl were bigger and I were smaller, it would be different between us. So I sat safely beneath it only because of the evolutionary quirks in our cycles.

A box-elder bug crept across the windowsill one afternoon, its cycle an aberration in the warmth of the house. It went from left to right, as purposefully as I punched the keyboard. We were there together, our cycles linked, and nowhere does it say that my cycle in the grand scheme rates higher than the bug's.

Dogs, creatures, neighbors, owls, bugs. The cycles are joined as in a great puzzle. There is no way to figure it all out. There is only time now, in the shadowy cave of winter, to acknowledge and ponder it, to know that this dim seasonal flickering is a time of leveling, of democratizing nature in our thoughts, and of coming to terms with our audacious consumption. And in that dichotomous exercise, we are left as legless creatures, condemned to squirm in our own company and saved—but only temporarily—from a hell of our own making by the simple awareness of what we are and what we are doing.

BUTTERFLIES IN A BLIZZARD

As you read this, a winter storm may be hissing at the windows, playing with your emotions as a cat with a mouse and daring you to challenge it, even for a second. And if the storm is not here as of this moment, it will be only a matter of time. Those of us who live in the northern parallels know all about that winter verity and face it with a mixture of dread and excitement. The storms will come. And they will dominate with the authority and unpredictability of schizophrenic gods.

In the first few snowflakes of the morning, there will be a whispered message: Make of this what you will, but we've got something planned here. Ignore us, and we will bury you. Prepare, and we will dissolve to nothing.

It is in such uncertainty that inconvenience and annoyance nestle like unhatched eggs, and death and disaster lurk like recruiting ghosts with quotas to meet.

And in that uncertainty is exemplified the ultimate rhythm of the earth, the exquisite unknown timing of beginnings and ends, without which our lives would be as regimented and dull as prison terms.

The winter storms highlight that impenetrable frontier for us. They will not be defined or duplicated, and in their contrary nature they sneak about like pranksters at a prom, and after a time they convince us to dance with our galoshes on.

It is a commentary on the fragility and vulnerability of our species that no matter the high level of our meteorologic sophistication, we still get caught by the winter storms, so that we end up cowering and shivering—or worse, freezing and dying. Arrogance does that to us. It denies us appropriate humility and makes it next to impossible to accept our natural place in the grand scheme. We have lived so long surrounded by little bubbles of artificial heat, and we forget that if something happens to the bubbles, we are as helpless as butterflies in a blizzard.

But years of conditioning are not totally lost on the "northern man" and his clan. Ultimately, he becomes sufficiently wary of the low-pressure curve balls that come sailing in from the direction of Colorado, and when the barometer plummets, he digs in to protect himself.

It is in that posture of preparedness that some of winter's finer moments occur. It must transcend species barriers and take us back behind that fork in the genetic trail, when we too hibernated. How else can you explain the intense feeling of comfort and well-being that consumes us when we are adequately supplied and sheltered as a winter storm begins to hiss and howl?

Then there is the air bubble standoff, and from the warm, cozy comfort, we can watch through the windows at the snowy swirl and bluster, and we can gather into ourselves like dogs turning in their beds or cats settling deeper into pillows.

But unlike the dogs and the cats, our instincts are susceptible to ego manipulation, and sometimes instead of staying by the fire, we go to meet the storm, confident of our invincibility and foolishly convinced of the importance of our mission.

If we do that and it kills us, the obituary should mention our stupidity, and we should be buried in a snowbank until the frost is out of the ground.

ALLIGATOR LUNCH

Strange little migrations, like the mindless scampering of car-chasing dogs, have occupied some of the populace in recent months. It is forever thus when the wind hisses down over the cold shoulder of the earth, and winter-gray shrouds the spirit of northern residents. Brief escapes are made—purposeless forays in the direction of the equator, where the "dumber" migrants have been basking for months.

In these respites, born of travel folder propaganda and impatience with such seasonal subtleties as skunk cabbage and premature pussywillows, the escaped northerner runs the risk of being burned in any number of ways. At the very least, he may find himself in an environmental situation that he did not bargain for.

So, in the tent, pitched amid the palms and the Australian pine on the banks of a brothy lagoon, the wild screeches from the other side of the canvas rent the night like the cries of demented pirates. "Bolt upright" is the cliche that comes to mind to describe the tent's heretofore somnolent occupants. It happened several more times before the sun brought relief as it eased up out of a bed of pink cloud pillows. A gallinule, a chicken-like bird also called a moorhen, had produced those outrageous night sounds, and it provided similar frequent outbursts during the day.

While the camp was not a living-off-the-land situation, the chicken-like gallinule was the object of dire thought and comment that would have it either fricasseed or fried before the sun went down.

That was the tone for the duration: that wild cackling in the middle of the night that was loud enough to wake the extinct Calusa Indians, then the daily grumbling and threats. One night, domestic chicken was grilled over charcoal within a few feet of where the gallinule spent most of its time. It did not take the hint: That night it was louder than ever.

Lofty philosophizing about the balance of nature and the unpredictable consequences of rude human intrusion did not carry the day, or the night. Memories of Aldo Leopold's sermonettes about natural harmony were as meaningless as the echoes of wedding vows in divorce court.

And then one evening a medium-sized alligator came drifting down the lagoon. It stopped in back of the tent and gave a hard-eyed look to its present company, its snout resting on the water like the chin of a grumpy desk sergeant, and its claws hanging down like guitar picks.

It was there when the last evening flight of pelicans sailed over the palm tops; it was still there when the daylight was gone and the lagoon was as dark as borscht. Its presence was not really threatening, but neither was it like having a friendly cat in camp. It is, of course, against the law to either torment or feed the alligators, so it was undisturbed as the campers went to bed.

Some time later, when moonlight was filtering down through the trees, there was a sudden screech and then a loud thrashing sound in the water. Again, "bolt upright" describes the tent scene, particularly with the earlier uneasiness generated by the alligator's visit. From just outside the tent, the beam of the flashlight showed the alligator's yellow belly and sides, glistening in the water like a new suitcase.

The writhing went on for several seconds, the water splashing up slowly as if it were heavy and thick; then the alligator righted itself and began to move off slowly.

It could be plainly seen: Clamped in the gator's jaws was the gallinule, its long, green legs protruding on one side and its wing tips on the other. It was dead and limp, and in the feeble flashlight beam, the alligator seemed to be wearing a satisfied expression.

But anthropomorphism is a hazard here. So, of course, is the assumption that a night of uninterrupted sleep for a misplaced human migrant is part of the balance of nature.

THE NIGHT WIND

The night wind comes out of the cold darkness with gossip as old as stone. It caresses the bare tree branches with slippery fingers and whispers of liaisons of the ages, of passions petrified beyond recall, of sighs from dark caverns.

The winter wind is a sound of nature that transcends the barriers of a society intent on isolating itself from the truth of its origins and its circumstance. There is no escaping it, and the wind makes its moaning points as authoritatively in the city as over the wooded hills.

The night wind's message can be anything: an eternal lecture from a despairing earth; the quiet wail of a system evolved beyond its capacity; the exquisitely edited record of the heretofore, as indecipherable as the hereafter.

The sound of the wind comes to all ears; then it does its unique slither and, like a fingerprint, it is different for everyone, curling inward to the marrow, slipping suddenly into a fracture of the psyche, pulling backward to challenge the gravity of time.

Now in the quiet of long winter nights, other sounds are remembered, and in that exercise the mystery of the id and the ages is compounded. The loon that called last summer on the wilderness lake can still be heard, its yodel and wail like an antidote for egotism. It came out of the starlit night as an invitation to the primordial party, and it carried the grand contradiction of forever denying acceptance.

Now the owls that called from the shadows of countless dusks are heard again—quavering, anthropomorphized inquiries that are silly as such, but laden with a communicative quality that stirs the bloody soup of evolution. The source of the sound—the fiercely glaring birds, all feathers and talons, are as invisible as spirits, and their calls come hesitantly, like something seeping up through cracks in the earth.

The geese of last fall, congregated in babbling gaggles, left such a residue of sound that it plays in the memory like an old theme song. The excited mix of honks and clucks and cries had risen up to become a chorus of ominous confusion, but in retrospect it hints of the magnificent orderliness, of an annual circulation and movement so exclusive that it cannot abide a species with the ability to question.

The outrageous screech of a blue jay sometimes bores to the quick of things. Like a dagger in a malevolent hand, it pierces the tranquillity of a winter afternoon for no good reason. It demands a response, but none can be dredged from the displaced mind, and it flounders in mute agony.

The musical gurgle of a raven in the solitary patrol of a frozen swamp becomes a painfully personal thing to the listener who is alone in the wilderness to hear it. It is stored in the audio file under "north," and it is as retrievable as the voice of a loved one who is gone.

The wild sounds touch and disappear, but never completely. The song of the coyotes that pursued something over the remote hills one bitter cold morning a long time ago can be resurrected as simply as you would punch up an audiotape. The excitement in the yips and howls was as palpable as the sting of the northern air, and a listener was paralyzed with the wonder and beauty of it.

Bigger wolves howl over this lonely land now, great wild canines of fierce independence, and that fact gives it a potential for majesty in the cacophony of nature's sounds. A calling to go there someday to listen becomes a sound of its own, and it grows with a slow and steady purpose, a siren song traversing levels of consciousness.

And in waiting to hear the arcane wild sounds that tease the hollowness where there may or may not be a soul, the common old night wind fills the void and speaks to everyone. It tells the story of community, of a joining so absolute and so vast that the distance between stars becomes minute. Then, in the darkness outside the windows and in the isolated spruce thickets, the sound of the wind is the same—the muted whispering of an indifferent universe.

EARTH'S BONES

Now in their nakedness, the trees stand as the framework for retrospective thought, their trunks and main branches as unyielding as convictions, and their bare, slender limbs as swayed by the day's vagaries as gossip-driven opinions. They are the rooted skeletons of botanic omnipotence, the earth's bones, at rest once more for an instant of winter.

There is a truthfulness about winter trees—an absence of pretense that says this is what we are at this seasonal moment, stripped of blossoming gaudiness and photosynthesis paraphernalia. We are this now—not like last year and not like next year—but this precise arrangement of cellulose that marches in place to the cadence called by the winds of this particular winter.

Taken collectively, the trees define the character of the earth's surface, and without them an absurdity and a sense of doom would set in—something unimaginable, like the final tide of a dying sea. As individuals, their shapes and configurations are so different as to mock the distinctive attributes of fingerprints.

The big oak in the back yard, for example, is like no other tree in the world. It is awesome in its solid attachment to the planet and in its strength of purpose, which is, of course, whatever it takes to survive. Its massive branches reach out over the house like the flexed wings of a great, malformed pterodactyl, and its roots have woven themselves into the soil for a century or more, until between the oak and the earth there would seem to be a rare synergistic guarantee of a future for all things.

On sleepless nights, the branches loom outside the bedroom window like the rungs of a misshapen ladder, propped against the moonlight and leading to an unearthly place of psychic incertitude. Once against the backdrop of dim, reflected light, a flying squirrel scampered over the dark branches, then was gone with a flick of its tail, like a bat in a dream.

To sleep beneath the tree's branches now, in the deep shade of the night, can be an anthropological adventure. The genetic memory is a will-o-the-wisp thing that answers to nothing, but the imagination can manipulate it until ancient ancestors materialize on the limbs as strange primates grinning in through the window.

On most of the earth's surface, it cannot be healthy to live a treeless life. It must at once produce stress and subliminal fear, since trees were obviously so intimately involved in the evolution of flight-or-fight as a survival mechanism. Remnants of that remain, as the occasional hunter or hiker climbs a tree to escape an attacking creature.

So where is comparable refuge for the generations growing up in the treeless, cornfield suburbs? They may not need trees to escape animal attacks, but where can they go with midnight reverie and random introspection when there are no tree limbs beckoning through the bedroom window? And what aberrations of ecologic judgment can we expect from these deprived people in the barren communities, and from those in the apartments stacked on top of one another until the view of trees is distant and perverted?

The backyard oak is showing signs of age. Several branches have ceased to function, and their bark is dropping off in dark scales. That circumstance may or may not have been exacerbated by the trauma from a house remodeling some years ago. The excavation certainly took some of the oak's roots, and that was unfortunate.

But our historic treatment of trees is fraught with such

abuse that we have callouses on our conscience, and only such catch phrases as "rain forest" and "old growth" get our attention, and then only fleetingly.

I am sorry for any damage I might have done to the oak. And now, as it stands strong and stark against the winter night, I am reassured only by the suspicion that it will outlast me, and someday someone else will look out through the bedroom window and see those ancient relatives perched on the bare limbs, staring like owls and grinning about the grand joke of it all.

The Centrifugal Force
of Cardinals

The cardinals have been trying to tell us something since way back in January. From the highest perches, brilliantly colored males have broadcast their piercing whistles with such authority as to make all other messages from whatever source extraneous and trivial.

The message is meant for other cardinals, of course, and it asserts: "Here I am! I like this place, and it is mine. I claim it in the name of procreation, the energy that drives all other energies."

To other listeners, however, the sharp whistling from the treetops says other things. To human ears, besieged by a cacophony of confusing messages from myriad electronic and mechanical sources as well as the haranguing of an army of hucksters, purveyors, politicians, and influence peddlers, the cardinal's message is a clear and simple declaration. It says that while the cold and ice may prevail, winter is simply a respite, a backing away from the frenzy, a time to breathe deeply, to reflect, and to plan; and that this "time-out" is as critical to the success of the annual cycle as the effervescence of spring.

The cardinal has expanded its territory in recent years, moving northward out of the redbird country of the south and setting itself up in new neighborhoods, where it is like a tiny flaming pilot light for the great seasonal fires of life that are to follow. Certainly a strong, loud whistle is useful in such matters.

It is in territorial delineations that everything rises and falls, lives and dies. It has been that way since the earliest slithering, and in the natural world there is an underlying harmony to it that is awesome in its dichotomous complexity and simplicity. Fifteen frogs in a ten-frog pond means that five frogs move elsewhere. Two birds on a one-bird perch dictates that one bird flies off to another tree.

This is a very basic natural fact, and nothing escapes it: too many people jammed into one place—into an aging, decaying city—means that suburbs sprawl out like something spilled, and the sprawl continues ad infinitum. The alternative is a nightmare, an uncontrolled eruption of concrete and steel that absurdly tries to define the species' sophistication by the height of its buildings and the concentration of artistic expression but is helpless before the savagery and bloodshed that gives a "stressed-rodent" quality to life.

The cardinal sings now for its own reasons, and only for other cardinals. It sings from a treetop that did not know a cardinal 30 years ago, and while it sings, it produces an old image of a Mississippi river bottom where the leafless underbrush, trimmed with the very first dogwood blossoms, was suddenly alive with dozens of fluttering redbirds. There were too many, it seemed. Too many focal points, and so many individuals that, for no good reason, the whole was greater than the sum of its parts.

Except under perverse and exacting circumstance— perhaps as muskox form a circle to protect their young— that is an intolerable condition in nature. The cardinals reacted to that instinctively, and over the years the flock flew apart from its own centrifugal inertia and the birds headed north with the resolve of explorers.

We hear them now, in the late winter dawns, those descendants of the Mississippi flyers, and we wonder at their apparent successful territorial expansion and their integration into new natural communities.

So for those questing souls who are forever groping

through personal and social fog, and who are not adverse to metaphoric excess, perhaps there is more to be heard in the cardinal's song. Maybe it is possible to hear a call to accommodate nature, to expand territory, to edge out of old ways and thought patterns and places, and to find a new perch from which you can announce your arrival with a cheery whistle.

CHILDREN OF THE SUN

In this gray time, this period of short, cold days between the long nights, parasites of the psyche stir, anxious, inquiring, ready to gnaw it all to dust. A vulnerability sets in, a susceptibility to languor and lethargy; depression threatens. In the low, thick clouds, spiritual vultures circle with their carrion appetites, and from the gloom of the wooded hills, there is a feral whimpering.

Now the land and its inhabitants have been abandoned by the sun, and there is a great writhing to survive. That all things are children of the sun is never more apparent than when the sun slides down on the horizon to reduce its angle of impact, and when it also disappears behind dense clouds for days at a time.

Other things live within cycles that adjust to this circumstance. The Baltimore oriole has gone at least as far as southern Mexico, and the nest it used last summer swings in the gray/white northern blizzards like a dirty snowball. Most of the oriole's colorful compatriots, and even the wild sparrows and blackbirds, have fled to warmer places, where the sun shines almost every day, and where cowering from the elements is not such a part of daily life.

Others creatures sleep, slowing metabolic rates until they are as moribund as fish on ice. From bear to chipmunk, the sleepers curl inward on themselves to protect the spark of life that ebbs to the very edge.

And in that highest form of life, in the featherless, peltless nakedness that must be an evolutionary joke for the members of our species living north and south of the tropics, you and I exist crab-like beneath the cold, sagging clouds of winter.

That we are clever enough to don clothes, shut doors and windows, and adjust thermostats gives us no solace in this season of gray; we have lived so long with our technology that our physical survival is as taken for granted as . . . tomorrow's sunrise.

But it doesn't rise, or at least it doesn't seem to, and therein is the rub. So we mope like spoiled children and we are not sure why, refusing to believe that we are so "natural" as to be at the mercy of something like the sun.

We put our technicians and our finest thinkers to it, and they say, "Yes, it is possible to become ill from a lack of sunlight, and this condition is called Seasonal Affective Disorder (SAD) syndrome," and for those who are severely affected, they recommend sitting under certain kinds of bright lights.

So is this the evolutionary answer to winter survival for our technocratic species? No migration, no hibernation, but rather sitting under artificial lights? The human absurdity goes on apace.

The sun! The sun! From 93 million miles away, it is the engine for all things on the earth, and when it teases us with its winter retreats we become confused and hurt, like children again, a little afraid and tending to congregate for protection.

For some—the authentic SAD cases—the artificial lights may be the appropriate antidote. But for the less severe cases—and that takes in most of us—it may suffice to keep in mind that the angle of the sun is changing even as we exchange these words, and though it may be hidden under clouds for days at a time, it will shine eventually.

That is the thing: It will shine. And when it does, seize the moment. Stop whatever you are doing long enough to acknowledge that if it were not for the sun, there would be nothing—least of all you and me. You might want to savor that verity in a park or a forest preserve, where the sun always seems to do its best work. Watch its first morning rays brush gold into the treetops, and pause later to see it glisten off the ice of a pond.

After so much winter gray, this exhilarating experience with the sun may move you to celebrate with a little personal song and dance. But be careful: The U.S. government outlawed the sun dance in 1904.

To Hear Nothing

It was one of those late-winter evenings when the pure silence of deep space descends to touch parts of the earth. In the ringing stillness, there was a breathless quality to the woods, a sense that the ending of this day portended more than just another twilight on yet another circadian cycle. There was the implied threat that, since it was perfect as endings go, tomorrow would be superfluous and is therefore cancelled.

In the fading light, in the freshness of the cold air, and in the magnificent quiet, there was a rare opportunity for sensory healing, a chance for personal receptors to lie as open as wounds, and yet to hear nothing, to smell nothing, and—with the ebbing of light—to see nothing.

A line of coyote tracks stitched through the crystal snow like punctuation for a previous night. The silent hunter had skirted the edge of a slough and slipped into the thicket, where earlier this day cottontail rabbits had dashed to hiding in the afternoon sunshine. The rabbits were there now, unmoving and unseen as this twilight deepened; and the hunters in the night would come to try to get them as certainly as the earth rotates to sink the sun: the coyote, foxes, owls.

It is the ultimate competition, but not competition at all—simply the exquisite natural harmony that takes in all things. And though it is conducted on a stage of continuous life and death, its drama is seldom seen and rarely heard. When it is the rabbit's time, it may depart with a brief scream of outrage, but that will be all, and then the silence will return deeper than ever.

That kind of silence—the absolute serene stillness of a late-winter, windless woods as night comes on—is as foreign now to modern life as the kerosene lamp. We live surrounded by so much noise that it is only when it reaches the thunderous levels of jet engines that we become concerned, or even aware of it. Our workplaces clatter and clang with machinery and buzz with computers. Our homes are cacophonies of loudspeakers, hums, bells, buzzes, and beeps. Our clogged streets are war zones of offensive decibels. We live with so much noise, in fact, that we are uncomfortable in its absence. We pipe music into every crack and crevice of our culture, and we clamp on earphones to guard against the possibility of even a second of imperfect quiet.

In addition to our other offenses against nature, we have become such a noisy species that the earth itself literally vibrates with our audio clutter.

Except sometimes in the woods, during the cold season of waiting when the day wind has sighed itself out and the black night is coming on soft, padded feet. Then the beauty of silence is as palpable as fireworks. It seems to come up out of the earth as a balm, like something precious that is stored to celebrate the end of noisy silliness.

So it was on the gentle slope just up from the slough. There, beneath the tall white pine trees, was that rare woods silence, as soothing and personal as old love.

It commanded a reverence, a motionless acknowledgment to make it perfect. And then, as the splendid moments passed and all things became one with the silence, it was suddenly violated by the liquid sound of distant church bells. The noise—for that is what it was— came as if electronically packaged and produced, and under the circumstances it was as offensive as the roar of a jet.

There can be no such thing as partial silence. Like pregnancy, it is either there in its totality or not there at all, and it doesn't really matter what destroys it.

The bell sound went on too long, and when it finally ended, it took a long time for the silence to reassert itself. When it did, its tenuous nature was apparent. It was like the rabbit in the darkened thicket where the coyote hunts.

So a silent scream of outrage went out across the wild land.

CROW MYSTERIES

You worry about the tumult and chaos in various parts of the world: I will concern myself with the trouble in the spruce trees. It has to do with the crows that roost there, and in its suddenness it is as mystifying as the abrupt collapse of foreign government.

Since the onset of cold weather, the crows have roosted in the tall spruce in an orderly manner, arriving singly or in twos or threes 30 minutes or so before dark and disappearing into the shadows of the dark boughs, where they spend the long nights as quietly as museum birds.

I don't know that each one chooses the same bough every night, but certainly they go into the same trees at the same height, and though there may be a dozen of them in one tree, you can walk beneath it in the bright winter moonlight and never seen a sign of them. It is as if they dissolve into the night to pursue some strange and unknown activity in different forms, perhaps streaking across the sky as meteors or flitting about the windows as the invisible painters of frosty designs.

Their disappearance into the spruce is a tranquil diurnal procedure that marks the time between day and night as certainly as the dying sizzle of the sun against the snowy horizon of the west.

And then one afternoon it all changed. First, instead of the quiet, late afternoon arrival of the birds in a slow trickle, there was a sudden squawking, cawing riot of crows in a nearby grove of oak. The cause of this uproar is unknown, though similar activity is frequently provoked by the presence of an owl. Whatever its cause, it was the kind of uncontrolled "crowd behavior" that would certainly panic any would-be avian peacemaker. It went on past the crows' usual early bedtime, and then the flock of wheeling, cawing birds dispersed, and individual birds began to drift over toward the roosting trees.

But there seemed to be a reluctance among them to do their usual disappearing act into the spruce. They sat about in the bare branches of the deciduous trees for a time, and only then did they slowly go to their accustomed nightly perches. All except one of them, and this one assumed a sentry-like position in the very top of a spruce. Then suddenly it launched itself into the fading light and vigorously pursued another crow off across the treetops. Their flight was a twisting, turning display of incredible aerobatics, and as they made the same precise movements, they looked like two great black bats after the same desperately fleeing bug.

The aggressor crow returned, and later so did the other one, and again there was a vigorous chase. The same thing went on yet a third time, and by this time it was nearly dark. But the first crow maintained its vigil in the very top of the spruce: Apparently, the second crow was not to roost anywhere nearby, even if it meant staying up all night to keep it away.

So I am left to ponder the situation. What was the crow riot all about, and did it have anything to do with the apparent ostracization of one of the flock? Was the crow banished from its accustomed roosting place, or was it a foreign crow trying to move in and snuggle next to another crow that was already spoken (cawed) for? And how was it decided which crow would chase the other one away? Furthermore, if one crow was simply mad at another crow, how long does a crow stay mad?

Serious questions all, and if you prefer them to some of the current international problems you might otherwise be considering, I welcome you to share them with me.

There is, of course, the possibility that since the crow nests so early—shortly after the snow is gone—what went on the other night was simply a display of crow jealousy, and could therefore be construed as the first sign of spring.

THE HAWK THAT CAME TO LUNCH

It was a special lunch on a bright winter day, when elegant sunshine topped the fresh snow and turned the world into a luscious visual dessert. The entrees were bird: sliced, smoked turkey on whole wheat for me, and breast of goldfinch for my companion.

The goldfinch was being devoured on my inadvertent recommendation, and there were some ambivalent feelings about that. The plan had been for the goldfinch to *have* lunch, not to become lunch.

But minutes after the backyard feeders had been replenished with thistle seed, there was a flash of wings and a heedless scattering of the small birds that had congregated. One of them ricocheted off a window; then it was suddenly in the clutches of a cooper's hawk that had come twisting out of the bushes like an aerial acrobat.

If the end had been as swift for the turkey as it was for the goldfinch, then the delegating of our predatory nature is well-served: A powerful clenching of its talons and a slicing blow with its sharp beak was all the hawk needed to turn the goldfinch into a prospective lunch. Then the crow-sized hawk that looked slightly blue and metallic in the brightness of the day flew to the rear of the back yard, with the goldfinch dangling from its talons.

The hawk landed on the snow and was very still as it surveyed its surroundings for several minutes. Then it moved onto the curved trunk of a honeysuckle several feet above the ground, and after another long pause, it began to prepare its lunch.

The turkey had come to my luncheon plate as far from being a bird as bacon is from being a pig. No feathers. No guts. No blood. No bones. Just a neat slice of meat, as easy to eat as a bread stick. It was that way because it had been passed from hand to hand by a virtual army of processors and providers, each one taking or adding or altering to transform a bird into lunch. It is the way of things in a complex society; not only have we lost the capacity to kill and dress our own turkeys, we forget that it has to be done if we are to eat birds—and/or animals, of course.

The hawk family has not traveled the evolutionary high road of delegation, and it must take apart its own birds. So the hawk began, holding the goldfinch in its talons and bending down to pluck the finch's feathers. For 20 minutes, it bent and grasped and pulled, pausing now and then to survey its surroundings. The feathers—only moments ago so precisely distributed and perfectly arranged on the finch, drifted down onto the snow and were as randomly scattered and lifeless as fallen leaves.

The cooper's hawk paused again, and then looked down at the de-feathered finch as any diner might pause to contemplate a lunch when it is served. Then the hawk reached down with its beak and began to tear off pieces of flesh, swallowing each one with a slight bowing movement of its head. In the expansive whiteness of the wintry world, the tiny pieces of finch flesh showed deep red against the hawk's plumage.

The bird ate with the neatness of a formal diner, dealing with each morsel carefully and completely before bending for another, and sometimes pausing between bites to sit as still as a judge.

Then its lunch was finished, and it wiped its beak on its perch and settled down into its feathers for some post-lunch relaxation. So, except for finding a roost for the night, the hawk had nothing to do until tomorrow, when it would have to catch another lunch. By contrast, those of us who lunch on processed turkey must get on with our complicated lives or there will be no lunch tomorrow.

The hawk seemed to settle deeper into itself, and then just as adieus were in order, a lone crow flew overhead and somehow spotted the resting hawk. Now, hawks may not have jobs, but crows do—and one of them is to torment hawks and owls until they leave town.

The crow gave its raucous alarm call, and other crows began to converge, landing in nearby trees and working from branch to branch down closer to the hawk.

If hawks could curse, this one certainly would have, as it ruffled its feathers, wiggled its tail, and turned on its perch to face away from the crows. But like the demands of a turkey eater's complex lifestyle, the crows could be put off for only so long, and finally the hawk flew into the shelter of a pine grove, with the crows in riotous pursuit.

Of all the billions of lunches on this winter day, the one with the hawk must have been one of the more fascinating. Tomorrow, a lunch is scheduled with an editor; it will not be nearly as interesting, unless, of course, the editor orders a live turkey, kills it with his bare hands, then plucks it with his teeth.

TIDES THAT BIND

Our long trek up from the sea and the present composition of our bodies has us aptly described as bags of salt water; and so it was appropriate to experience the tides on a recent night, when the moon was full and as close to the earth as it ever gets.

On this night, however, after some brief early glimpses when it shown like the porthole to a brilliant hereafter, the moon was obscured by clouds. But some of its light filtered through and served to mute and soften the darkness of the woods.

The snow underfoot had a wet-sugar consistency, and there was the inexplicable sound of dripping water, as if the maples were flavoring the night with a sprinkle of sweet sap.

The creek was bank-full, and it twisted black and serpentine in its sandy bed, carrying the cold blood of a dying winter back to the sea and the rocking of the tides. The stream ran with a soft gurgle, and the filtered moonlight glistened on its surface to give it the sheen of a mysterious lava flow.

Along the back trail, where the thick pine shaded out the muted moonlight, an animal—probably a deer—fled, its unidentifiable form going from shadow to nothing, and its movement marked by an indistinct crunching over the sugary snow.

Then, from the edge of the woods, the yellow windows of a farmhouse blinked across the fields, and off in the distance the glowing lights of small, invisible towns reflected against the purple clouds in faint orange bruises.

There was a sensation of tides, then, of people ebbing

and flowing across the land, of birth and death, of the salt water within and of the old man who died long ago and who came from the farmhouse to this precise place to wrestle with the trees for dominion over the sandy soil. All things have tides: It is only in something as big as an ocean that we are sophisticated enough to measure them.

Back in the woods, the moonlight dimmed, and a gentle breeze stirred the tallest white pine. And from high above, there was the sudden swish-swish-swish of powerful wings, as a nervous turkey left its roost and flew off into the night. The turkey's flight—skinning through the treetops in the pale moonlight—was a tide of its own, in which the bird did what was necessary to survive into the breeding season that was only weeks away.

That, of course, is the way of all living things—doing what is necessary to survive in order to propagate. The turkey's flight, the animal fleeing in the shadows, the old man who came to claim the land, the people in the little towns beneath the orange glows—it is all a great meshing of individual and collective tides, in which the ebb and flow is surviving and propagating.

At the stream again, the clouds had thickened, and the flow of the water was even more obscured and transformed. Now it was a black metallic artery of the larger world as it slipped away into the alder and dogwood, and it carried the omniscient reminder that just as we came from the sea, so shall we return there. One day, when the individual spark goes out and the elemental breakdown commences, the turkey and the fleeing animal and all of us who are mostly water will ride the creeks and the rivers back to the great seas, to be soothed again by the awesome power of the tides.

In the meantime, there is only a walk in the night when the pull of the moon's gravity draws the blood up onto trackless mental beaches, making you wonder how the old man's trip is going.

MILLONS OF WOMBS

The womb is not a bad place to be now, as late winter swaggers about in fits of uncertainty and depression. Within its warm confines, millions of fetuses are nourished and sustained like pampered royalty. Incredibly complicated cell arrangements are made. Umbilical cords, sophisticated conduits beyond the imagination, function with the efficiency of downspouts. And the wonderful warm bath in amniotic fluid is flawed only in that it is denied to consciousness and memory.

Within millions of wombs now, creatures build things in their own image, exquisitely formed and properly equipped to carry on the species.

Already there has been some emergence from the sanctuary of the womb. Tiny black bear cubs that would fit into teacups have made their exits and now snuggle against the mammary systems of somnolent mothers, waiting for spring.

But for the most part, the next generation of creatures is still womb-bound, its presence there dictating behavior to countless mothers-in-waiting. The fox vixen has found a sidehill burrow hidden away from prying eyes and the snooping noses of farm dogs. Bitch coyotes have done likewise; there is no howling at the moon in their lives, but rather a sneaking about to become as invisible as possible before the big event.

Female groundhogs, having accepted the overtures of males in early February, give themselves to the meaningful sleep of gestation.

The womb of the squirrel is full of the litter that will be born sometime later this month. That fact does not appear to seriously inhibit the female squirrel's limb-leaping activity, and the occupants of her womb experience action and thrills they will never know about.

Doe deer, as big-eyed and big-eared as caricatures, begin to bulge gently with their fetal burdens. The doe is one of the wild creatures that has the ability to practice survival "abortion." If the doe experiences nutritional distress early in her gestation period, she absorbs the embryo back into her system, which of course makes it absorption instead of abortion.

But this does not happen often. It is more likely that the opposite will be true: There will be sufficient nourishment to enable the doe to produce twins, or even triplets.

The badger, a flat-faced and aggressive burrower with bear-like claws, is another species with an unusual reproductive characteristic. The egg was formed in its womb back in August, then development was turned off until January, when it resumed in preparation for an early-spring birth.

So now the action is in the womb, superbly orchestrated in a kind of rare but common symphonic silence that is taken for granted by all of the creatures— including man, whose fumbling climb up the big ladder has freed his reproduction from the influence of the seasons and made it difficult to be appropriately humble before the wondrous biologic panorama.

The Snowstorms of Youth

It came late in the winter, but it was one of those Christmas-card snowfalls: big, fluffy flakes coming down in gentle swirls and building up in a soft layer over everything. To us—country kids headed for the little white schoolhouse—the snowfall was like a spiritual frosting on top of our boundless energy and innocence.

The snow commanded us like an itch, and we cavorted in it with the kind of abandon known only to children: climbing the snowbanks, leaping off into the drifts, shouting, falling, and rising to twirl away to the wild, cold music of the swirling snowflakes.

Once inside the schoolhouse, we sat damp and steaming, our brains as flushed as our faces. Caught up in the circumstance of the snow, we were as dumb as eggs; God Himself could not have taught us much.

Through the bank of windows to the east, we could see the snow coming down, thicker, it seemed—as if it would bury us in the schoolhouse and condemn us to an eternal hell of multiplication tables and geography.

By lunchtime, the snow was knee-deep and it became a grand adventure. A white force was invading our world, and though we knew some of its varied ways, we were wary of it. What were its outer limits? Just how far would it go in its threat to bury us? Was there an ominous note in the falling snow when you looked straight up and saw the shifting, gray, tunnel-like endlessness of it?

In the early afternoon, the teacher was defeated by the hopelessness of her task, and perhaps by the frightening prospect of being snowbound with a bunch of squirming, wet kids. She stood by the windows and watched the snow, and we all joined her.

The snow fell so thickly that it drew a curtain all round us and isolated us from everything. We could not see even the nearest farm buildings.

Then as we watched, out of the thick, gathering gloom and whirling snow, our fathers began to emerge, some driving tractors and some, like my father, guiding a team of horses that pulled a sled. It was like watching a great magic show, and from our uncomplicated youthful souls, cheering prayers of gratitude were dispatched silently.

The sled drawn by my father's horses was full of fresh straw, which could not disguise the fact that it was used frequently to haul manure. But that didn't matter. It was a wonderful ride over the hills, the horses' heel chains jingling and the sled bobbing up and down as if it were running over frozen waves. Then, at the end of it, there was the warmth and comfort of home.

It seems impossible to believe that in this day of incredible technology, a person of my tender years can revive a snow memory that involves horses. But time flies like the fragile snowflakes. It swirls briefly and then is gone.

And eventually, everything melts away, as the snowstorms of our youth rage in glory.

**If you enjoyed THE RIVER IS US,
be sure to ask for these fine nature books,
published by NorthWord/Heartland Press:**

The Land Remembers Collector's Edition by Ben Logan. Lavishly illustrated with color photographs, as well as photos from the author's family album, this is Ben Logan's classic remembrance of growing up on a Wisconsin farm during the Depression era.

Brother Wolf by Jim Brandenburg. We have hated the wolf. We have admired the wolf. Some of us have even loved the wolf, but few have known the wolf's story. With a powerful narrative and 140 remarkable photographs, Brandenburg reveals the mysteries of northern Minnesota's elusive timber wolf. *Brother Wolf* will revolutionize our thinking about wolves, human nature, our primeval past, and the survival of our planet.

The Barney Years by John Rucker. Once in a great while, the relationship between a man and a dog assumes heroic proportions. *The Barney Years* is one man's search for a meaningful life on the land, a life-and-near-death journey across Alaska, Montana, Canada, the Dakotas, and North Carolina. The author's traveling partner is an extraordinary springer spaniel: Barney.

True North by Stephen J. Krasemann. What would it be like to spend a year living in the northwoods? Author/photographer Krasemann answers the question by living that year on the reader's behalf, and by capturing the true nature of the North Country in words and images.